THE
STORY
OF
THE
RING

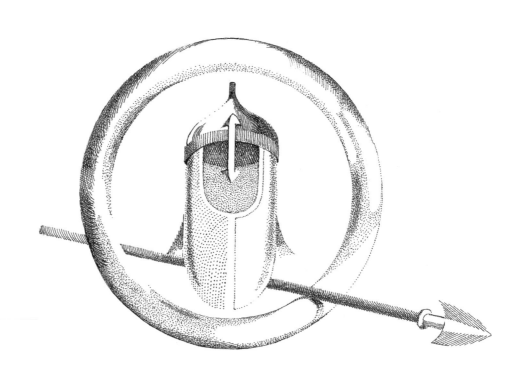

THE
STORY
OF
THE
RING

WAGNER'S *DER RING DES NIBELUNGEN*
RETOLD BY MICHAEL BIRKETT
ILLUSTRATED BY ELIZABETH BURY

FOREWORD BY PETER HALL

OBERON
BOOKS
LONDON

First published in 2009 by
Oberon Books Ltd
521 Caledonian Road, London N7 9RH
Tel: 020 7607 3637 / Fax: 020 7607 3629
e-mail: info@oberonbooks.com
www.oberonbooks.com

A catalogue record for this book is available from the British Library.

ISBN: 978-1-84002-938-3

Book design by Jeff Willis.

Printed in Great Britain by
CPI Antony Rowe, Chippenham.

CONTENTS

Working provokes creativity more than familiarity. Michael Birkett has been my friend for nearly 60 years and still regularly upstages me with his stupendous knowledge. For instance, he continues to understand far more of Wagner's *Ring* than I manage – and I've only tried to direct it.

It is easy to lampoon the doings of this famously divine and dysfunctional mountain-top family but a proper understanding of the libretto's intricacies is vital to enhance our appreciation of the music. Michael's version is clear, it is lucid and it is a model of modern English prose. The story unfurls as a compelling epic to which all ages can respond.

On a Sunday afternoon, as my wife and I drove away from one of Michael's famous lunches (lunches at which Wagner was vigorously chewed over) I had a sudden idea: I knew who could give life to Michael's text, for his book needed illustrations.

'I know who should illustrate.'

My wife chipped in:

'I know who you're going to suggest.'

'You can't know…'

'One, two, three…!'

'LIZ BURY!'

We were in unison. Elizabeth Bury, an inspired and subtle creator of theatrical sets, costumes and props, is also a considerable artist and brilliant draughtswoman.

With her husband, John, she collaborated on many great productions. John died in November 2000, but his austere, rigorous vision remains influential all over the world in designs for operas, plays and theatre buildings.

Happily, a single telephone call sufficed to persuade Elizabeth out of retirement to participate in this project. Within a year, she had produced all the iconic images for Michael's text. Bold and evocative, they bring us nearer to Wagner. They make us, indeed, ready for the music.

So here is the book: created by Michael, made eloquent by Elizabeth and beautifully realized by the publisher, James Hogan.

Sir Peter Hall CBE
September 2009

I have retold this immortal tale out of frustration. I am tired of reading that the *Ring* Cycle is a masterpiece so impenetrable that it requires research and expertise to unravel it. Nonsense. The story is of exemplary simplicity and clarity and can be understood by adults and children alike. Of course it is long; it is a saga which lasts in the opera house something like fifteen hours, depending on who's conducting. But it is no more difficult than the Brothers Grimm or Charles Perrault or Hans Christian Andersen.

Of course, once the musicologists come in, everything changes. The retelling of the tale by Wagner himself is immensely complex. The music, with its network of interrelated leitmotifs, and even the libretto, which makes use of the ancient alliterative verse form *Stabreim*, repay all the study and the analysis which the story itself does not require.

I hope you will read the story for its own dramatic sake, whether or not you are planning to sit through all four parts of the *Ring* Cycle in the opera house. Even if you are, a knowledge of the story will make the experience clearer and more enjoyable.

Michael Birkett
October 2009

THE
RHINEGOLD

(Das Rheingold)

Alberich lusts after the Rhinemaidens

nce upon a time, long before the world that we know, there was an ancient realm. Through it flowed a mighty and spellbound river, the Rhine. Hidden deep within that river was the most valuable treasure ever known – the Gold of the Rhine. Seemingly unassailable, it was guarded by three water-nymphs, luscious as fruit and slippery as fish – the Rhinemaidens Wellgunde, Flosshilde and Woglinde.

Beneath the bedrock of the Rhine lay Nibelheim, a dark, cavernous kingdom peopled by the dwarvish Nibelungs. One day an evil creature crawled out of Nibelheim and up to the river; it was Alberich, the most powerful and the most evil of the dwarfs. He was captivated by the alluring Rhinemaidens, and even though they were repelled by his savagery, they in their vanity and self-regard could not resist teasing him. Again and again his lust drove him to clamber up the slippery rocks to where the maidens were gracefully darting and diving just out of his reach; again and again he slipped and fell back, unable to catch them.

The theft of the gold

As the sun struck the Rhinegold it threw spears of golden light that shimmered through the river. Catching sight of the gold, Alberich was instantly consumed by a different kind of desire. Settling back into the shadows of the river's bedrock he gazed at the treasure, listening to the prattle of the Rhinemaidens.

Complacent in their vanity, the maidens continued to tease Alberich. 'Why, in the gold's lustre you are almost handsome!' they laughed. 'What is this treasure that glistens and gleams so brightly?' he asked the Rhinemaidens. 'Have you not heard tell of the Rhinegold?' they replied.

'He who possesses the Rhinegold,' said Wellgunde tauntingly, 'if he should fashion a ring from it, that ring would give him dominion over all of the world's sovereignty and wealth.'

'Hush, Wellgunde!' said Flosshilde. 'Are we not charged with protecting the Rhinegold from those who would steal it?!'

'We need not worry, sister,' replied Wellgunde. 'Any man who would take possession of the gold must first forsake love, must curse love itself. This dwarf is so lewd and lustful, we have nothing to fear!'

Alberich dives back to Nibelheim

Alberich, inflamed by their scorn and crazed with greed for the Gold, suddenly issued that terrible curse: 'Love, from this moment forward I denounce you!'

Catching the Rhinemaidens off guard he leapt forward, wrenched the Gold from the rock and plummeted to Nibelheim. As his cruel, mocking laughter echoed around them the Rhinemaidens fled, shrieking with guilt and terror.

Wotan and Fricka awake to Valhalla achieved

High above the river, on a mountain so lofty that it almost reached the sky, out of sight of Nibelheim, the gods were anticipating the completion of their great castle.

Wotan, father of the gods and the most feared being of all the universe, slept on the mountainside with his wife Fricka. As Fricka awoke, her eyes fell on a wondrous sight: the castle was completed, their monumental work achieved. Waking her husband, she pointed to where their palace and fortress stood gleaming in the sky.

No sooner had they celebrated their triumph, however, than they heard heavy footsteps approaching. Fasolt and Fafner, giants of the middle earth, had built the palace for the gods, and had come to collect their promised payment – Freia, sister of Fricka and the goddess of Springtime, keeper of the magic orchard whose golden apples contained the secret of the gods' eternal youth. Fasolt in particular had been captivated by Freia's radiance, the only warmth that might transform his savage existence.

The giants demand their wages

Fricka was outraged at the bargain struck by the male gods. 'Are you so hungry for power,' she demanded of her husband, 'that love and familial ties mean so little to you?' But Loge, Wotan's servant and the demi-god of fire, was secretly aware of a more serious problem with Wotan's pledge to the giants. The gods depended on the golden apples that they picked daily from Freia's orchard for their power and immortality.

Partly driven by lurking resentment of his inferior status and Freia's reluctance to give him her fruit, Loge himself had advised Wotan to agree the contract. When the time of reckoning came, he had suggested, he would devise a way out of the bargain. Now, though, as the terrified Freia appealed to Wotan for protection, the king of the gods knew that he was bound by his pact, carved as it was as a sacred rune into the shaft of his all-powerful spear.

At first, Wotan pretended that the bargain had been made only in jest, but the giants furiously objected, holding fast to the terrified Freia. Her brothers, Froh and Donner – gods of Spring and of Thunder – threatened the giants with battle. But Wotan knew that the bargain was fast. 'No battle,' he insisted. Freia and her brothers began to despair.

Freia, the hostage of Riesenheim

As the gods turned towards him, gazing on him in mute suspense, Wotan stood fixed in a torment of indecision. Catching sight of Loge, he turned his rage on his servant. 'You by whose malevolent counsel this bargain was struck, why are you silent now?'

Cool and sly, Loge stood firm. 'Were it not for me,' he said, 'your castle would never have been built! In your moment of need it was I who devised a solution to your problem. Now, once again,' he confided, 'I have found a ransom to take the place of Freia, one that the giants will not be able to refuse.' He told Wotan and the gods of the Rhinegold and its great powers, and of Alberich's bold theft. That gold was the only ransom which the giants would prefer even to Freia. Wotan must steal it from Alberich.

A pale mist began to fall over the mountainside, and, without Freia's precious apples, the gods began to appear grey and old. Once again they turned to Wotan. Feeling the weight of their expectation he knew that he must descend to Nibelheim and snatch the Rhinegold from Alberich.

As the giants hauled the terrified Freia away as a hostage to their cold and muddy kingdom of Riesenheim, Wotan forced Loge ahead of him as he made the descent to Nibelheim. Fricka, Froh and Donner remained on the mountain-top, where they awaited Wotan's return.

The descent to Nibelheim

In the cavernous gloom of Nibelheim, Alberich was discovering the magical powers of his stolen Gold. Even with all his cunning and guile, Alberich did not possess the necessary skill at the forge to fashion the Ring of which the Rhinemaidens had spoken. He had ordered his feeble-minded brother Mime to produce it, and now he dragged him by his ear from his place of toil. 'Have you not yet forged me my ring as I commanded? I will pinch you until you are black and blue if you have not!'

'I have!' shrieked Mime. 'Loosen your grip!'

'Why, then,' demanded Alberich, 'do you not give it to me?'

Mime had witnessed the power of the gold whilst forging the ring, and weary of his brother's dominance had also fashioned for himself a helmet that enabled its wearer to assume any form or disappear from view. As Alberich wrestled with his brother the Tarnhelm fell from Mime's grasp. Snatching it up Alberich turned on his brother: 'Would you trick me?! Do you think that you will keep my treasure for yourself?' Placing the Tarnhelm on his head Alberich became invisible and set upon his brother, who shrieked and cowered as he found himself thrashed mercilessly by a disembodied whip.

Setting the newly forged Ring upon his finger Alberich assumed absolute power. He enslaved the whole race of Nibelungs and set them about searching for more gold in every cleft in the rock that he might increase his vast hoard.

The trick – Alberich as a toad

When Wotan and Loge emerged from the sulphurous clefts into Nibelheim they found an arrogant, gloating Alberich towering over a cowering, terrified Mime. Loge affected awe in the face of Alberich's new-found dominance, and Alberich could not resist demonstrating his powers, setting the helmet on his head and transforming himself into a gigantic worm. Loge professed that he was dumbfounded with fear at the apparition, but cunningly hinted that it would be more difficult, even impossible, for Alberich to transform himself into something small, like a toad.

'Nothing easier!' boasted Alberich, who immediately pronounced the spell and turned himself into a tiny hopping toad. At this, Wotan and Loge leapt forward and grabbed Alberich, who by the time he had regained his usual shape was roped hand and foot like a slave. His captors bundled him up the sulphur cleft to their mountain plateau below Valhalla, still enveloped in the grey mist that had fallen on the ageing gods. There they demanded as ransom for his freedom the gold of the Nibelungs.

Filled with rage and shame in his bondage, Alberich had little choice. He summoned his legion of dwarfs to bring up the Rhinegold. Mortified at being seen by them in such abject captivity Alberich bid them leave the gold before wielding the Ring and banishing them again to their caverns.

Having relinquished his treasure Alberich now demanded his freedom. With the Tarnhelm and the Ring, he thought, he could easily regain his power. 'You have your ransom,' he said to Wotan and Loge. 'Might you not,' he asked, gesturing to the Tarnhelm which Loge still held, 'return to me my helmet? Even as a gesture of kindness?'

'You have not yet,' retorted Loge, 'been punished for your theft. The helmet will act as your pardon,' and with that he tossed it onto the pile of Rhinegold.

'Curse you!' snarled Alberich. Still, he thought to himself, he had his Ring. 'Untie me, you tyrants. I have given you my all. Set me free.'

'You have not,' retorted Wotan, 'yet given your all,' for he had observed the effect of Alberich's Ring upon his Nibelungs. 'What is it that gleams upon your finger? Does that not also belong to the hoard of the Rhinegold?'

'Do not,' begged Alberich, 'take my Ring. I would rather give you my life!'

'"My Ring"?' snorted Wotan. 'It is no more your Ring than is the rest of this plundered gold,' and with that he set upon Alberich and wrenched the Ring from his finger. 'Now,' said Wotan to Loge, 'you may set him free.'

Alberich's curse

Alberich greeted his empty freedom with a howl of rage and fury, and pronounced a terrible curse upon the Ring, so powerful and so deadly that it resounded through the lives of gods, dwarfs, and men for generations.

'Whoever touches it shall be wracked with pain and misery. Whoever has it shall be eaten up with worry. Whoever has it not shall be eaten up with envy. Everyone shall lust for it. No one shall enjoy it. Its master, no matter how strong his defence, shall draw his own executioner to him. Doomed, he shall be driven by terror. The master of the Ring shall be its slave, until once more the Ring be returned to this my hand from which it was stolen.'

As Alberich scuttled away down to Nibelheim, the mists cleared. Fricka, Donner and Froh emerged, anxious to know if the ransom for Freia had been secured. Even as Wotan proudly pointed to the Gold, the giants were heard thundering across the wasteland. Seeing the golden hoard that awaited them, they set Freia free.

Fafner kills his brother

The giants immediately set about dividing their Gold between them. Fasolt, however, desolated at the loss of Freia, insisted that the Gold be piled high enough to hide her from his sight. Wotan commanded Froh, Donner and Loge to do so. But even after every ingot had been added to the pile, the heartbroken Fasolt complained that he could still see a glimmer of Freia's hair above the rampart of Gold.

'Throw that thing onto the pile,' he shouted, gesturing towards the Tarnhelm. Loge dashed forward to defend it, but Wotan commanded that he let it go.

'I can still glimpse her eye through that crack' he cried. 'Fill it up.'

'Nothing left,' replied Loge.

'Wrong,' said Fafner, gesturing towards Wotan's finger. 'There's that Ring.'

'My Ring?!' said Wotan. 'My Ring is not for ransom. It is rightfully mine, the spoils of victory in combat.' The Ring that gave him unlimited power and dominion over all, this he could never give up. With it, surely he could turn back the course of the gods' ageing. Surely nothing would be impossible for him so long as he possessed the Ring.

Angrily Fasolt pulled Freia back to him from behind the gold. As Fafner appealed to Fasolt to stay and fight for the gold, the gods appealed to Wotan to hand over the Ring and save Freia, their kinswoman and the source of their immortality.

Without warning, darkness descended and a handsome, majestic woman emerged bathed in blue light from one of the rock clefts: Erda, mother of the earth, younger than the springtime of Freia but older than the runes of Wotan's spear. It was Erda's daughters, the Norns, who spun the endless web of fate. Erda was not merely the repository of all earthly knowledge: she was Knowledge itself. She was Wisdom and she was Prophecy.

'Give up the Ring, Wotan!' she intoned. 'Its great power conceals a foul curse. All-seeing and all-knowing, I have come to tell you of the dread destiny that you bring upon yourself and your kin if you do not relinquish the Ring.'

Wotan was deeply shaken. He cried out to know more, but Erda had vanished. Crazed with desire to know and control his destiny, he began to pursue Erda into the earth, but Froh and Fricka restrained him. 'Stay, Wotan!' they begged. 'Heed Erda's warning!'

Subdued by their appeals, Wotan sank into reflection. After a moment he roused himself, grasped his spear and turned to face the giants.

'Come to me, Freia,' he commanded, tossing the Ring onto the pile of gold, and the giants released her.

Immediately the giants set upon the gold. Fafner spread out a gigantic sack and started pitching treasure into it for himself. Fasolt objected, appealing to the gods to see fair play. Loge, cunningly seeing an opportunity, advised him to keep only the Ring and to let the rest of the treasure go to his brother. Hearing this, Fafner seized upon the Ring and in the furious struggle that followed killed his brother Fasolt.

'Now you may dream of Freia's gaze,' said Fafner savagely, 'but the Ring sees you not!'

Wotan ignores the Rhinemaidens as the gods stride into Valhalla

Wotan and the gods were horrified to observe how swiftly, and in what a welter of blood, Alberich's curse had been fulfilled. As Fafner's gigantic footsteps thundered away across Riesenheim, the huge sack of Gold banging and clattering over his shoulder, Wotan looked into the future with dread.

Gently, though, Fricka reminded him of their shining new citadel. The mists still shrouded it, but Donner, swinging his huge thunder-hammer, called up a storm and the mists scattered. His brother, Froh, flung a bridge of frozen rainbow across the chasm between the earth, with its rivers, plains and clefts, and the castle, with its immortal glittering grandeur. It rose up, shining in the light of the setting sun, waiting for the ceremonial entry of the gods. Turning to his wife, Wotan solemnly said, 'Come with me now, wife, and dwell with me in Valhalla.'

'What does this name mean?' asked Fricka. 'It is unfamiliar to my ear.'

'When the course of our fate has unfolded,' Wotan replied, 'when I have acheived all that I dream of and desire, then you will understand this name.' Then he took his wife's hand and turned to lead the gods into their new home.

As the gods crossed the bridge in triumph, the Rhinemaidens far below wailed for their stolen Gold. Pausing, Wotan listened to them for a moment in irritation. 'Cease their complaint,' he ordered Loge, before resuming his stately passage into Valhalla.

'They are marching to their doom,' muttered Loge to himself. 'They are assured of their majesty, but I feel nothing but shame to be with them. Sometimes I desire nothing more than to transform myself into flame and consume them utterly. Who knows what I might do…?'

But Loge followed the gods as they marched over the Rainbow Bridge into Valhalla. The trumpets sounded. Their dream was fulfilled. Their fate was sealed.

THE VALKYRIES

(Die Walküre)

Sieglinde finds Siegmund, exhausted by his escape

ccording to the treaties and contracts engraved on the shaft of his spear, Wotan was ruler of the gods and had dominion over giants, men and the Nibelung dwarfs alike. He had, however, etched a foolish contract into that sacred spear, pledging as payment for his towering new citadel the goddess Freia, whose fruit was the source of the gods' immortality. Forced for their survival to provide a substitute payment, the gods had little choice but to hand the powerful and cursed Rhinegold to the giants Fasolt and Fafner, rather than returning it to the protection of the Rhinemaidens. With Alberich's curse upon it, the Ring fashioned by him from the Rhinegold promised mastery of the world to those who would forswear love. That curse had taken immediate effect when Fafner had killed his brother Fasolt in his greed to possess the entire treasure.

By means of the Tarnhelm Alberich had transformed himself into a monstrous and fearful dragon, and now he guarded his treasure in a dark cave in the depths of the forest.

The tribes of the earth, all of them seeking the mastery of the Ring, were locked in conflict, the pursuit and slaughter of their enemies the only way of life that men knew.

One day, as a storm raged, a young man took flight from a fierce battle. His spear and shield had been shattered and splintered and he could no longer fight. He found shelter at the edge of a forest, but his enemies were not far behind, and fearing their wrath he ran on and on, further and further into the forest, seeking a safer place to hide.

The deeper he plunged into the forest, the darker fell the sky and the colder the rain. Barely able to see before him, he staggered on until he was so exhausted he fell to the ground, gasping for breath. He could go no further. For now he was safe, his enemies far behind, but what lay ahead? 'What hope have I here,' he sighed, 'of finding food and warmth and a safe place to sleep?'

At that moment he noticed a glimmer of light through the trees. Wearily, summoning his last effort, he staggered to his feet and lurched towards it. In a clearing he found a strange hut, built around the trunk of a towering Ash tree. Craving rest, the young man staggered into the hut and sank to the floor by the fire, falling instantly into a deep slumber. A young woman emerged from the shadows. She was shocked to find a stranger lying on her hearth, but having assured herself that he slept soundly she cautiously approached him, observing his battle wounds and his battered dress.

Suddenly the man started and awoke. 'A drink!' he cried out. 'I must drink.' The woman filled a drinking horn with water and offered it to him. As he raised it gratefully to his lips and drank, he began to take notice of her radiant beauty, her kindly face glowing in the firelight. 'Who is it,' he asked, 'that I must thank for this hospitality?'

The woman told him that she was wife to the warrior Hunding, master of the house. Her husband would certainly give shelter to a wounded warrior, she told him as her eyes looked with concern upon his injuries.

'My wounds are but slight,' the young man insisted, springing to his feet. 'If only my spear and shield had served me as well as these strong limbs of mine! Now, as a result of your great kindness, my energies are renewed and I must leave you be.'

'Rest a little while longer,' pleaded the young woman. 'Let me bring you

Siegmund's story

some reviving mead,' and she refilled the drinking horn. 'Let it touch your lips first,' asked the young man, his admiration for the woman growing by the moment. Each gazing fixedly upon the other, their emotions in turmoil, the two took turns to drink from the horn.

Sighing deeply, his eyes sinking to the ground, the young man rose to his feet. 'I must leave,' he told her. 'Who is pursuing you?' asked the young woman. 'Why are you in so much danger?' 'I am ill-fated,' the young man replied. 'Ill-fate pursues me wherever I go, and will overtake you as well if I stay here too long. I have found peace here for a short while, but now I must leave lest I bring misfortune upon you.'

'You should stay, then,' she replied. 'Misfortune has already made its home here.' Even as she said this the door burst open, and there stood Hunding, master of the house, his spear and shield still ready for battle. Shocked and suspicious at finding a strange man in his home with his wife, he noticed as he exchanged the rough courtesies of hospitality how alike they were. 'They have the same serpent's glint in the eye,' he said to himself.

He asked the young man how he had found this house, hidden so deep within the forest. 'I fled so quickly from my pursuers,' the young man replied, 'that I hardly know from whence I came.'

'I am Hunding,' said the warrior. 'In return for my hospitality trust me with your name.' But the young man replied that he scarcely knew what his name was – 'It must be a woeful one,' he said, 'because my life has been so.'

'If you will not tell your story to me, stranger, then tell it to my wife. Look how she longs to hear it.' And so, as the woman gazed upon him, the young man began to relate his adventures to Hunding and his wife.

'My father, Wolfe,' said the young man, 'was the only person I have ever really known.' His mother had been slain and his twin sister, he thought, had perished when a savage tribe called the Neidings had burnt their home to the ground. He had lived like an animal in the forest with his father until the Neidings had launched a fierce attack upon them, such that he was separated from his father and never saw him again. All he had found of him had been an empty wolf skin. Craving the company of men and women he had left the forest, but everywhere he went he was an outlaw. He met nothing but anger and disdain, caused nothing but sorrow and strife. 'Every good action of mine was counted as ill, while everything I recognized as evil was greeted by others as benevolent.'

'The Norn that wove your fate cared not for you,' said Hunding as he noted the sympathy with which his wife gazed upon the stranger. 'You should not be welcomed as a guest by any man, perhaps, lest you bring your own sad fate to bear upon him.'

'Only a cruel and cowardly man could fear an injured and unarmed man,' retorted the young woman. 'Tell us,' she asked the stranger, 'of the most recent battle in which you lost your weapons.'

The stranger told them of his fight for a defenceless girl, who had appealed to him when her kinsmen had tried to force her into a loveless marriage. For hours he had battled her oppressors until her pitiless brothers lay dead and the girl herself stalked the battlefield weeping for the very kinsmen who had enslaved her. He had defended her against her clan until his weapons were hacked from his hands,

Siegmund tears the sword from the Ash tree

but his last sight of the battlefield had been that of the girl herself, lying slaughtered upon the heap of bodies he had left.

As he listened to this story, Hunding suddenly rose up with fury. 'I am a kinsman of that clan,' he thundered. 'I too was summoned to the battle but came too late. Nothing is sacred to you and your kind. Tonight, by my obligations of hospitality, you will shelter in my house, but tomorrow we will fight, and you shall pay me for my kinsmen's blood!'

'Away,' he ordered his wife as she attempted to move between the two men and avert their quarrel. 'Prepare my nightly drink and wait for me in my bed-chamber.' Hesitating for a moment the young woman departed, and Hunding swept after her.

Left alone in front of the fire, a stranger indeed the young man felt himself to be. He had stumbled exhausted and defenseless into the house of his enemy. His father, he recalled, had promised him that in his hour of direst need he would find a sword. This, surely, was the hour, but where was the sword?

Something glistened for a moment in the last light of the dying fire, something embedded in the trunk of a great Ash tree whose massive roots grew downwards through the floor and whose branches towered up through the roof. Distracted, that gleam recalled to him only the effect of the young woman's gaze as it rested upon him, so bright and intense that it seemed to him like the sun which had never shone upon him. As if drawn by his thoughts, the girl hastened into the room. She whispered to him that she had drugged Hunding and urged him to flee under cover of night, to save his own life.

'But you, you are my life!' he cried with passion and ardour.

'Oh, would that you might make this weapon your own,' she exclaimed, showing him where a huge sword lay buried in the trunk of the Ash tree. She related the story of her own unwilling marriage to Hunding. At the wedding feast, she told him, whilst Hunding and his kinsmen drank, she had sat sad and alone. Suddenly a stranger had entered – an old man in grey, his hat hung down over one of his eyes, but the other gleamed so fiercely that all the guests feared him. Only to the girl herself did his look seem kindly – under his gaze she felt a sweet, sad yearning. He had swung this huge sword in his hands and then buried it up to the hilt in the trunk of the Ash tree; it should belong, he decreed, to the man who could pull it out. Every guest to their house had tried, but none had succeeded. Now, though, she realized that only the noblest of heroes could ever draw the sword out of the tree, a hero who would atone for all her shame, grief and suffering. And this stranger, she hoped in her heart, was that hero.

The young man clasped her to him, crying out with joy and triumph. Two desperate and loveless souls, together they had found glory. As they half-whispered, half-sang their love to each other, the girl began to feel that she knew his voice of old, from childhood even.

'Are you truly named for sorrow?' she asked. 'Can you not take the name of joy?'

'Call me what name you will, I take my name from you,' he replied.

'But your father's name was that of the wolf?'

'Only to cowardly foxes.' The young man then revealed what he had known in his heart since they had first looked upon each other: 'My father's real name is the

Wotan and Fricka – the eternal conflict

same as his whose eye shone so proudly on you at your wedding feast – Wälse!'

Then the girl realized that she was both sister and destined bride to this young man. They were both Volsungs, children of Wälse. This was indeed the hero for whom she had waited, for whom the sword had been embedded in the great Ash tree. She named him Siegmund and herself Sieglinde – brother and sister of victory.

'Nothung!' cried out Siegmund, naming the great blade that his father had buried for him so many years before. He reached up for the hilt, and tore the sword in its dazzling brightness from the trunk of the Ash. Siegmund and Sieglinde fell into each other's arms, and the blood of the Volsungs was united.

The next morning dawned pale and stormy. On the eternal heights, overlooking the world of men, stood Wotan, sacred spear in hand, armoured from head to foot, his gigantic four-winged, eight-hooved warhorse beside him.

In order that he might protect himself should the Nibelungs ever regain control of the Ring, Wotan had enlisted the help of the nine Valkyries, the daughters borne to him by the Earth Mother, Erda. He had charged his Valkyries to gather about him in Valhalla an army of great warriors; they swooped in on scenes of mortal combat, snatching great warriors as they finally fell to their fate and carrying them off to the castle of the gods. What Wotan needed above all else, though, was a hero who had grown up without the help of divine intervention and who was therefore not bound by any of the treaties that bound Wotan. It was with this destiny in mind that he had fathered Siegmund and Sieglinde under the name 'Wälse', and secretly he had watched over their fate.

Siegmund, he knew, if Wotan were to exercise his secret influence, might come into possession of the Ring himself, and save the earth from its terrible fate.

Wotan called to Brünnhilde, chief and his favourite among the Valkyries, to join him. Foreseeing a battle between Siegmund and Hunding, Wotan charged Brünnhilde with bringing victory to Siegmund. Brünnhilde happily agreed, dashing quickly away over the rocks to avoid Fricka, Wotan's long-suffering and embittered wife, who was rushing towards them in her chariot.

So angry was Fricka, as she swung her thick golden whip, that the giant rams that pulled her chariot were groaning with terror. Wotan knew well enough what it was that had brought Fricka to this pitch of fury.

'You will not,' she screamed from her chariot, 'decree victory for Siegmund! He is a vassal and a slave, he is guilty of incest, and he is the product of your adultery! If you intervene on his behalf you will be dishonouring me, the holy vows of marriage, the sacred runes and treaties of your spear and the gods themselves!'

Wotan wearied of these arguments. Fricka, he thought to himself, worshipped what was old, established and honoured by time, like the ancient vows of matrimony. She could not, like him, grasp their destiny until it unfolds. The Volsungs, he told her, were united by love, and love he could never condemn. He argued that the love of a brother and sister, bold though it was, had never graced the earth before. He argued that their own courage was worthy enough of respect and alliance. He argued that Siegmund had found and won his bride and his sword, unaided.

But Fricka was implacable. There was no freedom of will, save by decree

Brünnhilde rebellious at her order from Wotan

of Wotan; no future, save what he predestined. Heroes and slaves alike were the creatures of Wotan's will. Would Wotan, the all-knowing and the all-powerful, permit the honour of his wife and of the sacred institution of marriage itself to be trampled on?

Fricka could not be appeased. Had she not followed Wotan's every footstep? With her all-seeing eye did she not know of every one of his infidelities? Did she not suffer agonies as he begat his Valkyries upon whichever woman stoked his lust? Did she not know, too, that Wotan had fathered the Volsungs, and with what cunning he had placed the sword in the great Ash tree and predestined their meeting?

From fury Wotan turned to pleading, but finally, as his works were exposed by his wife, he yielded. Siegmund should fall in the battle. 'Let him be free,' he pronounced. 'I will not protect him. The Valkyries will ride free, doom or save as they wish.'

Fricka strode away in triumph and met Brünnhilde approaching again. 'Now,' she crowed, 'ask your father how the battle is to fall.'

Brünnhilde approached the shattered and despairing Wotan. She had never seen her father look so care-worn. Wotan, though overflowing with the grief of the world, still hesitated to pour his heart out to a daughter, but Brünnhilde's passionate concern and affection for her father released the flood of his emotions.

All his immortal life, Wotan told her, he had been torn between lust for power and for love, with their unpredictable and equally passionate lusts. Since his creation of Valhalla, paid for with the ill-gotten gold of the Rhine, he had been haunted by Alberich's curse. When Erda, omniscient Earth Mother, had risen from the earth

to tell Wotan of the evil power of the Gold, she had given warning but refused him any prediction. Pressed by Wotan, she had simply vanished. Tortured by the conflict of his limitless power and his hopelessly limited vision, he had driven downwards, through the earth's crust, found Erda, tamed her, charmed her and fathered on her his favourite of all daughters – Brünnhilde.

Then had Erda revealed to him her vision – his nightmare – that the gods would founder and Valhalla crumble. This would happen when Alberich – he who had abjured love – should produce a son. Now, Wotan confessed to Brünnhilde, he had heard that Alberich had indeed conceived a son, conceived not out of love but hate, born, or soon to be born, of a woman seduced with Alberich's gold. Worst of all, born of a woman once wooed in vain by a loving Wotan, but won and made pregnant by the hate-filled Alberich.

Brünnhilde reminded him of the great halls of Valhalla, which Wotan had filled with heroes to be his defence against Alberich's black hordes. But Wotan knew that if Alberich ever regained the Ring with its power of dominion, Valhalla's heroes would betray Wotan and fight against him in the ranks of darkness. Then would Erda's vision be realized. Having relinquished the Ring as payment for Valhalla he could not retrieve it without rejecting love, and losing the essence of his power and immortality. 'The covenant by which I rule,' he told Brünnhilde, 'is the covenant that binds me.'

Only one who had not been exhorted and protected by Wotan, a lone hero fearless and brave, acting of his own noble accord, could avert the doom and destruction of the world.

Brünnhilde warns Siegmund of his death

Was not the Volsung, Siegmund, such a man, pleaded Brünnhilde?

But Wotan knew in his heart that Siegmund was not, for he himself, a god, was Siegmund's wolf-father. Wotan, disguised with his hat pulled down over his missing eye, had watched over Sieglinde and driven the sword into the Ash tree for their protection. Now that Fricka had exposed his deception all hope in Siegmund had died.

'This is now your battle order,' pronounced Wotan to Brünnhilde with a heavy heart. 'Siegmund the Volsung is to die.'

Brünnhilde refused. She rebelled. She knew, better than her father, his secret heart. She would never slay his son, never obey the darker side of his conflicted will.

Wotan blazed with fury. 'What are you,' he demanded of Brünnhilde, 'except the blind tool of my will? Beware of my anger. You have never seen the ultimate wrath; it can turn smiling joy into smoking desolation. Siegmund is doomed. That is the task I lay upon you and upon all Valkyries.'

Brünnhilde had never seen her father so angry, and yet so shaken and despairing. Something of his despair gnawed into her own spirit, and she went into battle, not brave and joyful as beforehand, but fearful and heavy-hearted.

Far below her, Sieglinde was dragging Siegmund along in a frenzy of terror. She was in the grip of a sudden and terrible vision from the very earth-bed of their bliss and so she plunged wildly into flight. Rock and cliff, field and river, she had crossed them all in a state of panic. Siegmund could not restrain her, as she shouted for him to shun her: she was dishonoured, she cried, accursed, already nothing more than a corpse.

Even as Siegmund tried to reassure her, Hunding's horns could be heard from afar and Sieglinde was raging again. She was in the grip of a vision so fearful that it drained her of all spirit. She saw Siegmund's great sword, Nothung, shattered into splinters, his body torn apart by dogs. She slumped to the ground, and Siegmund helplessly cradled the desperate creature in his lap.

Brünnhilde, far above, saw the couple twined about each other and set her winged horse, Grane, to soar down to a rock beside them. Softly she called to Siegmund and he raised his eyes in wonder to the warrior-maiden towering above him, shield and spear sparkling in the dawn light, her giant war horse motionless beside her. 'Who are you,' he asked, 'that you look on me with such solemn beauty?'

And so Brünnhilde revealed to him his destiny. Only those destined to die gloriously in battle, she told him, looked upon her face. She had come to lead him to Valhalla, the house of the great war-father. Siegmund asked if he would see this great war-father in there? And would he see his father Wälse? Brünnhilde promised that he would. He would join the throng of heroes and be waited on by the wish-maidens of the gods.

'And shall Sieglinde, my sister and my bride, be with me in Valhalla?' he asked. 'No' said Brünnhilde. 'Sieglinde will remain on this earth.'

At this Siegmund fixed his gaze calmly on Brünnhilde. With the deepest gravity he said, 'bear my greetings to Valhalla, to the great war-father and to my own father Wälse. Bear my greetings to all the heroes and to the wish-maidens. I shall not be following you there.' Brünnhilde told him that the die was cast: he had looked on her

The ride of the Valkyries

face, and this was his doom. But Siegmund found no terror in her face. He would stay beside Sieglinde for good or ill.

Brünnhilde told him she had come to announce his death in battle against Hunding. Siegmund laughed at the threat. Had he not a great sword, and was not victory predestined by it? Brünnhilde revealed that the sword's maker had rendered it powerless and allotted to him not victory, but death. Siegmund was outraged. He poured scorn on the treachery of the creature that promised a victorious sword and then betrayed that promise, and on the ice-cold heart of the Valkyrie who stood before him. If this was the meaning of Valhalla, he would rather go down to Hell. Brünnhilde was astounded and touched. Did Siegmund care so little for everlasting bliss and so much for one mortal woman?

Siegmund, in a frenzy of grief, threatened to kill both Sieglinde and himself. Overwhelmed by his great passion, Brünnhilde contradicted Wotan's order by promising Siegmund victory. She would reverse the tide of battle, she told him, and fight for him against the decrees of the war-father.

Siegmund heard Hunding's dogs and his horn sounding across the valley and found Sieglinde blessedly asleep. Had the Valkyrie brought her such peace, he wondered? But Sieglinde's sleep was not peaceful at all. As Siegmund strode away, shouting defiance at Hunding, with Nothung shining in his hand, Sieglinde's mutterings suggested memories of a terrified childhood: where was her father, where was her brother? The house was in flames, where was her mother? Mother!

Her nightmare became reality as she awoke to see Siegmund and Hunding locked in a fight to the death. As she

rushed towards them, her figure was dwarfed by that of Brünnhilde, urging Siegmund to strike the fatal blow with his sword. But in a blaze of thunder Wotan appeared and towered over them all, his gigantic spear reaching down to the earth. As Siegmund struck, Nothung shattered on that immortal shaft and Hunding drove his own spear clear through Siegmund's defenceless body.

Sieglinde screamed and swooned. Brünnhilde, aghast at Wotan's sudden arrival, rushed to Sieglinde and lifted her, unconscious, onto Grane's back. Mounting her great horse she carried the young woman away into the cover of the gloom, leaving Wotan on the battlefield with his lifeless son and a victorious but terrified Hunding.

'Slave!' intoned Wotan to Hunding. 'Kneel before Fricka, and tell her that Wotan's spear avenged her disgrace. Go!' But Hunding slumped, lifeless, his heart stopped by fear. Wotan turned his war horse towards the fleeing Brünnhilde, and with a great oath full of fury and retribution soared after her.

Far below the mortal slaughter raged on, and the Valkyries snatched up heroes destined for Valhalla. With enemies so deadly and so newly slain slung over their Valkyrie saddles, even the war horses reared and snapped at each other in the confusion. As the armoured Valkyries called to each other and the pile of the favoured dead grew, they realised that one of their number was missing. Calling out to Brünnhilde they spied her in the distance, Grane gasping with extertion as she plunged him into woodland close by. There she dismounted and sank to her knees.

As they approached her, the Valkyries were astonished to find that across Grane's

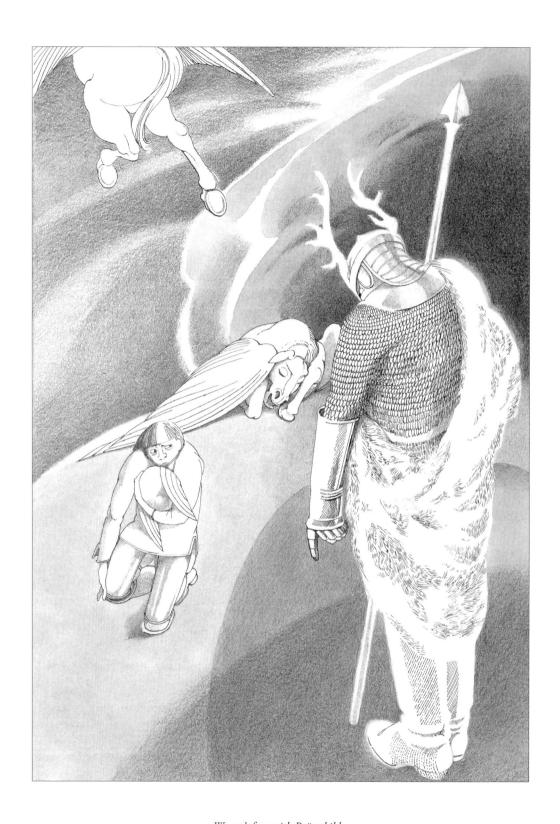

Wotan's fury with Brünnhilde

saddle was slung not a dead warrior but a living woman. Brünnhilde told them the story of her part in the Volsung battle, and that Sieglinde must be saved. She warned them of Wotan's thunderous approach, and already her sisters were aware of a huge black storm-cloud gathering. They urged Brünnhilde to deliver up her prisoner: none of them would dare to defy Wotan. Brünnhilde begged them to lend her the swiftest of their horses to bear Sieglinde to safety, since the avenging Wotan would slay her as a Volsung, but none of them would do it.

Sieglinde could bear her grief no longer – she cried to Brünnhilde that she would rather die with Siegmund. She cursed her salvation and begged the warrior-maiden to plunge her great sword through her. But when Brünnhilde revealed that Sieglinde was carrying Siegmund's son her despair changed to ecstasy. Brünnhilde gave her the shattered fragments of Siegmund's sword and prophesied that one day the son she carried would be a hero worthy of the name of victory – Siegfried. Sieglinde blessed Brünnhilde and swore to keep safe her son who would one day smile upon Brünnhilde. Then she dashed away into the cover of darkness.

By now the storm bearing Wotan had reached the rock, and the Valkyries huddled round Brünnhilde to hide her. Wotan in fury strode towards them, knowing that Brünnhilde was within their terrified circle. The Valkyries beseeched him to be calm, to show pity to their sister who had begged in her anguish for their protection. Wotan was pitiless in his anger and scorned their terror. Was this the courageous band of women he had created? Where now were their iron wills and brave hearts? Did they know what an unforgivable crime Brünnhilde had committed? She alone knew his most secret thoughts, and these were her commands. Did they not know that it was she of all of the Valkyries that made Wotan's vision reality?

And did they know that this same Brünnhilde had betrayed his secrets, defied his decrees, broken the bond between them, and turned against Wotan the very weapon that he had lovingly forged for her alone?

Now Wotan's fury turned upon Brünnhilde herself, for hiding in so cowardly a fashion from justice. 'Do you think,' he thundered, 'that you can escape your fate?'

No sooner had he uttered the words than Brünnhilde stepped out from the protecting circle of her sisters. 'Here am I,' she said. 'Tell me of your justice.'

'Your punishment is not mine,' replied Wotan: 'you made it yourself.'

My will it was that made you;
your will has turned against me.
My commands were your only duty;
Your commands have turned against
   me.
You were my wish-maiden;
Your wishes have turned against me.
You were my shield bearer;
You turned my shield against me.
You cast lots for me;
You have cast them against me.
You fired my heroes;
You have turned their fire against me.
What you were I have described,
What you are, you have decided,
Wish-maiden you were, once,
Valkyrie you are no longer
What you are is henceforth only what
   you are.

Wotan's heart melts

Brünnhilde's bravery and defiance were now exhausted and a heavy sense of doom settled on her as she realised that her father spurned her. Wotan confirmed only too clearly all her fears: she would never again know the heroes of the battlefield; never again ride with them into Valhalla; never pass the battle horn to her father and be kissed in return. She was no longer of the gods, not of their company. She was no longer even of her father's house, utterly banished.

Brünnhilde and her Valkyrie sisters were appalled that Wotan should so brutally snatch back every power and every gift he had ever given her. 'Not I, but a stranger,' said Wotan, 'shall take those things from you. For I shall lock you under a spell in a deep and defenceless mortal slumber, here on this bleak mountain. The first man to find you, and wake you, shall have you.'

The Valkyries were now beside themselves with horror: Brünnhilde's shame and dishonour would fall upon them too. They shrieked at Wotan to withdraw his curse. But Wotan's fury was unstoppable. Had they not understood? From now on Brünnhilde's womanhood would be at the mercy of a mortal husband. So far from riding through the sky as a Valkyrie, she would sit spinning wool by the fireside and be little more than an object of mockery.

Brünnhilde swooned under the weight of Wotan's malice. Her sisters instinctively recoiled from her, and Wotan mercilessly turned their distress into terror. If any one of them should think to befriend her sister, or stay to comfort her, then she would suffer the same fate as Brünnhilde. 'Get away from her this instant or you are doomed,' he roared, and the whole flock of Valkyries, wild with fear, tore from the cliff-face of the mountain in a frenzy of plunging hooves and thundering wings.

Distant lightening lit for a moment the tumult of their flight, before the dark clouds settled again over the mountain. Brünnhilde, slumped at her father's feet, slowly opened her eyes. A great silence seemed to surround the two solitary figures.

Alone again with her father, Brünnhilde asked him questions to which both knew and dreaded the answers. Was her crime so shameful that she must be shamed, so disgraceful that she must be disgraced and so dishonourable that she must be dishonoured? 'Tell me,' she insisted as her spirits revived, 'of the guilt in you. Nothing else could make you so savagely reject a child you once so deeply loved.'

The shaken Wotan repeated gloomily his resentment that his commands should have been disobeyed. But Brünnhilde had seen deeper into Wotan's heart than he himself had dared to look. She knew of his overwhelming love for the Volsungs, for Siegmund and Sieglinde. She knew that it was only his burdensome and bitterly resented duty to Fricka that had made him order Siegmund's death.

She told him of Siegmund's inspiring rejection of her pronouncement of death and transfiguration and of how she had thrilled to the love and the sense of honour that seemed to shine out of him. But at this Wotan's bitterness overflowed. 'You luxuriated in a dream of love and passion,' he rasped, 'knowing all the while that I was condemned to reject all that I loved, all that I most passionately cared for. I had to think of the salvation of a whole world, whilst you thought only of the salvation of your own affections.'

'Perhaps I loved better than you ever could,' replied Brünnhilde. 'I understood

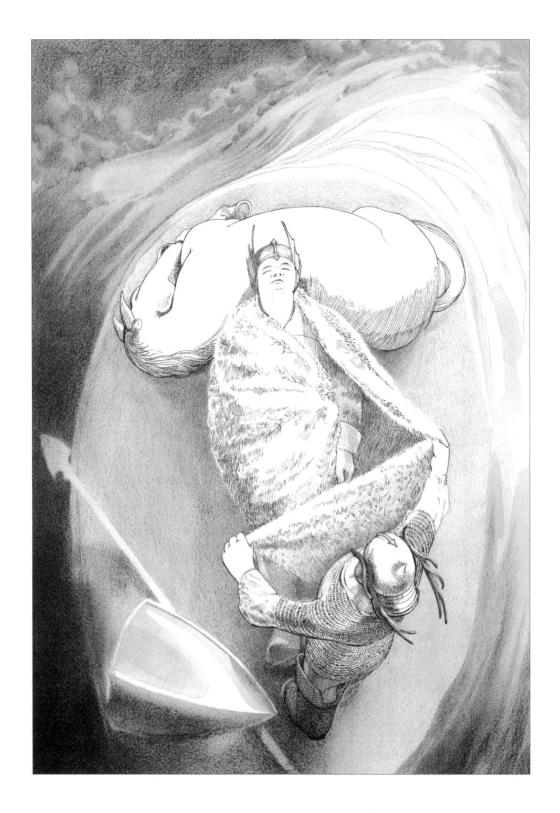

Brünnhilde in her ring of fire; Wotan in his endless vigil

and obeyed your commands not simply by your words but by your heart. I am too much a part of you not to know your secret voices. The dishonour you believe you must put upon me, you will put upon yourself.'

Wotan sourly reminded her that if she had always responded only to love, then henceforth she must reserve that love for a husband.

'You must not sacrifice me to any cowardly mortal!' she exploded. 'Only to a hero should I be bride! You could never breed a coward but only a Volsung; a Volsung will come to claim me.'

'Do not speak to me of the Volsungs,' pleaded Wotan. 'They had to be destroyed, they were exterminated by envy.' Gently Brünnhilde told him of Sieglinde's survival, of the son she would bear, and of the sacred splinters of his sword Nothung.

'Do not forget it was I who splintered it,' growled Wotan. 'They can expect no protection from me.'

But fast as Wotan might hold to the inevitable, perhaps predestined, punishment of his daughter, yet Brünnhilde's determination to maintain her pride and her spirit, rooted as they were in a god-given code of honour, seemed to grow in strength. She begged not to be offered as prey to the meanest of predators but only to a hero worthy of her.

But the fate of the Volsungs was fresh in Wotan's mind – he had grown weary of trying to people the world with his own offspring. 'You ask too much,' he muttered.

Brünnhilde flung herself round her father's knees in one last, ecstatic burst of defiance. 'Then ring me with fire,' she demanded, 'a fire so fierce that only the most fearless of heroes shall ever find his way to my desolate rock!'

At last the floodgates opened and Wotan's pent up affection for his dearest but doomed daughter burst out of him. 'You brave and wonderful child. It shall be as you wish. I bid you farewell forever, but you shall have such a bridal fire as was never seen before. A fire so bright it shall strike terror into mortal men. But your own bright eyes that I have loved so much, those eyes that have so often promised hope and happiness, they shall not see the fire. Now I kiss your eyes into a long enchanted sleep, and that kiss drains your own divinity. When your sleep is over, you will awaken to mortality.'

Brünnhilde was already deeply asleep in his arms. Very tenderly he laid her down beside her sleeping horse, Grane, on a bank at the summit of the mountain. He closed her battle-helm and covered her with her great war-shield. For one long moment, filled with infinite pain and sorrow, he stood looking down at her. Then he strode down the mountain side calling for Loge, the fire god, conjuring him by all the spells by which he was bound to Wotan to raise the magic ring of fire, and striking three immense blows on the rock with his spear.

The hill echoed like thunder to the blows, and the mountain exploded into fire. The giant ring of flame blazed like some terrifying portent of the world's destruction. Above it, in perfect silence, slept Brünnhilde. And below it, in perfect silence, stood Wotan with his gigantic spear. Very slowly, the stars began to glow.

SIEGFRIED

(Siegfried)

Siegfried terrifies Mime with his bear

The towering circle of fire on the highest peak of the mountains had blazed uninterrupted for almost twenty years. Far, far below, in one of the immense forests that covered the plains on either side of the great river Rhine, was a cave from which came the strangest sounds. A constant, almost frenzied hammering would be followed by silence, and then equally frenzied shouting and screaming.

It was the home of a dwarf and a handsome boy, just on the threshold of manhood. The boy was called Siegfried, and the dwarf was Mime, the evil brother of the even more evil Alberich. It was Alberich who had stolen the gold of the Rhine from its keepers, the Rhinemaidens, and Mime who had forged from it the Tarnhelm, which gave anyone who wore it the gift of invisibility, and the Ring which bestowed on its owner the much-desired but ultimately poisonous gift of absolute power. The gold, the Tarnhelm and the Ring had been stolen from Alberich by Wotan, most powerful of all gods. Alberich in his fury had placed a terrible curse on the Ring. But in turn Wotan had been forced to yield it, and the rest of the gold, to Fafner and his brother Fasolt as a ransom for Freia, the goddess of youth, who had been promised as payment when the giants had built Wotan's fortress Valhalla. Fafner had slain his brother Fasolt and with the help of the Tarnhelm turned himself into a huge and fearsome dragon. The gold had been hidden away in a cave, and Fafner the dragon lay at the mouth of this cave guarding it day and night.

The dragon is the clue to all the hammering and shouting from Mime's cave. For Mime wanted the dragon's gold. And he knew that young Siegfried had the courage and the strength to kill the dragon. But only the great sword, Nothung, could do the deed. He, Mime, had neither the courage nor the strength. But he was the wisest and craftiest smith ever. So every day he tried to forge the unbreakable, the invincible master sword. And every day Siegfried came home from the forest, tried the new sword, and in one mighty stroke, smashed it into pieces like a toy.

By now Mime's confidence in his own skill had vanished, and the satisfaction of a craft deftly exercised had given way to a sense of drudgery, and a life that seemed both hopeless and purposeless.

One day, Siegfried returned home from the forest driving before him a huge brown bear. Mime was dreadfully afraid, Siegfried vastly amused. 'Gobble him up,' shouted Siegfried. 'Gobble up the hideous little smith who can't make a sword. Ask him where the sword is, Bruin.' 'It's here, I've finished it,' cried Mime in his terror. 'Bad luck, bear,' said Siegfried, 'he has saved his skin for today. Off you go.'

Mime showed him the new sword and declaimed, as always, about how bright and sharp it was. And Siegfried, as always, knowing that brightness and sharpness are nothing without toughness, picked up the sword and smashed it down on the anvil. As always, it shattered into a thousand pieces.

Then followed the shouting and screaming which the forest had learned to expect after the roaring of the forge fire and the hammering of steel on anvil. Siegfried shouting in frustration that Mime kept boasting of his prowess as a swordsmith, and foretelling heroic deeds and mighty battles, and then producing weapons so puny and fragile that he simply crushed them in his fist. And then threatening to crush Mime in the same way.

And then Mime protested about the boy's ingratitude. How he brought him up, fed him and nursed him, made him clever and ingenious toys, even made him his hunting horn. And about the wisdom he taught him and the gratitude he should show. But no, nothing but indifference and ingratitude. Siegfried roamed the forest to his heart's content, whilst Mime stayed at home like a slave. His reward? Hatred.

Then, more quietly, Siegfried began to ask the questions that really troubled him. He had watched the birds and beasts of the forest and had learned what love might look like. Always a pair. The mother suckled, the father fed. So where was Mime's wife? Where was Siegfried's mother?

Mime, as so often, dodged the issue; Siegfried must think of him as both father and mother. But Siegfried had looked into a forest pool and he had been struck by how little he looked like the hideous Mime. Didn't children always look like their mothers and fathers? Mime might have fed him and cared for him, but father he could never be. Now suddenly he knew why, however often he escaped from his loathing of Mime and made off into the forest, he always returned again. It was to discover who his real parents were.

Scarcely had Mime tried to ignore this last sinister question when Siegfried had him by the throat. 'Tell me my mother's and my father's names. Why must I throttle you before you will tell me anything? I almost had to strangle you to learn to speak.'

Mime, in genuine fear of his life, finally confessed that he was no kin to Siegfried. He had found his mother in agonised childbirth and helped her into his cave. Beside his hearth she had given birth to Siegfried, though she died in the delivery. Siegfried looked ready to strangle him

again. 'And why am I called Siegfried,' he asked? 'It was your mother's name for you. She said it would make you handsome and strong.' 'Then what was my mother's name'? for a moment Mime pretended to forget and for a moment Siegfried seemed ready to spring. 'She might have been called Sieglinde' stammered Mime. 'And my father's name?' shouted Siegfried. 'I never knew him, never saw him,' shouted Mime. 'Your mother just said he was slain, she left you here – but fatherless!' Something told Siegfried that this was, for once, the truth. But something made him insist on knowing one thing more. 'I never trust you with my ears,' he said. 'I can never believe what you say. Show me, before my eyes, some pledge, some sight of the truth.'

Reluctant and shifty as ever, but still terrified of the now electric tension in Siegfried, Mime slowly revealed the shattered fragments of the sword, Nothung. 'Your mother gave them to me for safe keeping,' he confessed. He laid the pieces of the sword before Siegfried. 'Your father carried this sword in his last fight, when he was slain,' he whispered.

It was as if Siegfried had waited a lifetime for this moment. 'Today,' he cried in a frenzy, 'you shall forge these fragments into a sword for me. Now, this instant, you shall start. Now is the moment to show your true skill. No cheating, no botching, or you will suffer for it. Today I must have the sword!' 'Why today?' stuttered Mime in panic.

'Because today I leave the forest, for the wide world. I shall never return, I am free. Nothing binds me here. You are not my father. Your hearth is not my home, your roof is not my shelter. Wherever is far from here, there is my home. Happy as a fish in the stream, happy as a bird in the air, lighter than the wind over the woods, I blow across the world. To see you, Mime, never again!' And Siegfried stormed out of the cave into the sunlit forest.

To Mime, the shadows in the cave seemed darker than ever. Siegfried was escaping from him, and without Siegfried what hope was there of conquering Fafner? Worse still, he knew with a deadly certainty that no skill of his, no tricks or magic that he had learnt in the forges of Nibelheim, could ever weld together the fragments of Nothung, the sword of swords.

And out of these very shadows came a tall gaunt figure wrapped in a huge cloak. One eye was covered with a blind man's patch. But the other glittered with almost unnatural brightness. A wide-brimmed hat was pulled down over his face and by way of a staff he carried a huge spear. 'Who are you?' cried Mime in alarm. 'They call me the Wanderer, and I have indeed wandered far and wide.' 'Then wander away' said Mime inhospitably, 'from these savage and desolate woods.' And he tried everything he knew to dislodge the stranger from his hearth. But the Wanderer told him of his wisdom, and of the help he had brought to troubled souls who sometimes neither knew of, nor understood, their perplexities. He invoked the laws of hospitality and flattered Mime for his wisdom. Finally he pledged his own head if Mime should defeat him in a wager of knowledge.

Mime could not resist the challenge, and devised a contest of three questions.

'First,' said Mime, 'Tell me what race it is that lives in the depths of the earth.' The Wanderer told Mime all that he knew already of the Nibelungs and of his dread brother Alberich, of the gold of the Rhine and of the Ring.

'Next,' said Mime, 'Tell me what race it is that lives on the surface of the earth.' The Wanderer told Mime all that he knew already of the Giants, of the death of Fasolt, and Fafner, transformed into a dragon, guarding the hoard.

'Last,' said Mime, 'Tell me what race it is that lives on the cloudy heights above the world.' The Wanderer told Mime all he already knew of the Gods and of the all-powerful Wotan, who had subdued both Nibelungs and Giants. And he told him of Wotan's all-powerful spear, hewn from the most sacred branch of the World Ash Tree, into whose shaft he had cut the runes and covenants of life, and with whose point he ruled the world. As he made this description, the Wanderer happened to tap the ground with his own spear, and immediately a roll of thunder echoed through the woods.

Mime hoped the Wanderer would go now. Instead the Wanderer told him that by the laws of wagering and the laws of hospitality, since he had pledged his head against three questions and redeemed it with his three answers, the dwarf must do the same.

Mime sensed dimly that Wotan's eye had somehow spied him out in his cave, and his wit sagged against it. But he could not resist the power of this stranger, and he knew he must submit to the three questions, 'First,' said the Wanderer, 'tell me what race it is that Wotan punishes worst yet loves the best.'

And Mime told the Wanderer what he knew already of the Volsungs, of Siegmund and Sieglinde, and of how they begat Siegfried. 'Next,' said the Wanderer, 'tell me what sword it is that Siegfried must wield if he is to slay Fafner and make the wise Nibelung, who watches over him, lord of the treasure and the Ring.'

Wotan and Mime – the question and answer game

And Mime told the Wanderer all he knew already of Nothung, and Siegmund pulling it from the Ash, and its breaking to pieces on Wotan's spear.

'Last,' said the Wanderer, and a chill of dread seemed to enter the cave, 'tell me what smith is it who will weld Nothung together from its splinters.'

And Mime told the Wanderer nothing but his own fury at being unable to forge the sword. 'Now,' said the Wanderer, 'your head is forfeit. You should have asked me what you most desperately needed to know. Instead you asked futile questions about far-off things. Now I reveal the secret: he it is who has never known fear shall forge Nothung. And he it is to whom I bequeath your doomed and forfeit head.' And the Wanderer swept almost silently into the forest. The only sound that remained was the echo of a long mirthless laugh.

Mime stared after him in dread, and suddenly everything in the forest seemed full of menace. Every mist seemed to be the breath of the dragon, every shimmering light the fire from his mouth, every crackle the snap of his jaws, every swishing the lash of his tail. 'He's coming for me,' screamed Mime, 'Fafner!' And he shot into the cave and dived in terror behind his anvil.

But the only real creature to emerge from the forest was Siegfried, shouting for Mime, shouting for his sword, shouting with all his boyish impatience. Mime emerged, trembling, from behind the anvil, his head still full of his terror of Fafner and the dread prophecies of the Wanderer. 'Are you alone?' he whispered. 'What are you doing behind the anvil?' asked Siegfried. 'Are you sharpening the sword for me?' But Mime was still muttering to himself: 'A sword? How can

I weld a sword? He it is who has never known fear. I have grown too old, too wise, to do it. But my wise old head is gambled away, forfeit to him who has never known fear.'

Siegfried neither understood nor trusted a word of all this. 'You're just trying to get away from me,' he bellowed. Mime cringed, 'Oh I could get away from anyone who could be afraid. But this child, I never taught him the one thing he should have needed. I tried to teach him love, love for me. But that was a failure. So how shall I teach him fear?'

Siegfried was so enraged by the dwarf's hysterics that he was on the point of strangling him, when Mime suddenly seemed to be seriously and deeply troubled. More important than forging a sword, he declared, was learning the meaning of fear. He, Mime, had learnt it, so that he could teach it to Siegfried. 'What is it?' asked Siegfried bluntly. 'You talk of roaming out into the wide world, and you don't know what fear is? I promised your mother I would never let you out into that wicked world unless you did!'

Siegfried could not understand why, if it was a craft, he had not mastered it. Mime tried to describe – to invoke – terror. But all he described was his own panic-stricken fantasy of a predatory and vengeful Fafner, and his own wildly hammering heart. Siegfried was intrigued: his own heart didn't hammer, but he was quite impatient to experience all these thrilling sensations. But how could a coward like Mime be his master in fear? Mime seized his chance. 'There is a dragon,' he said. 'This dragon has killed and eaten many good people, and if you follow me to his lair he will teach you the meaning of fear all right.' Siegfried

The forging of Nothung the sword

immediately wanted to know where this lair was. 'Neidhöle' said Mime. 'To the East. On the edge of the wood.'

'Not far from my world then' said Siegfried. 'So that's where you can lead me, as soon as I have learned fear and you have forged the sword. Where is that sword?'

Finally Mime had to acknowledge that he had neither the vision nor the skill to weld the fragments of Nothung together. Siegfried, as if predestined for the task, proclaimed that he himself would forge anew his father's sword. And immediately he set about transforming the forge. What had been cramped and cluttered became broad and clear. What had been hot, became molten. Siegfried threshed the bellows into action, and the fire blazed with incandescent flame. 'What is the sword called?' shouted Siegfried. 'Nothung' screamed Mime. Dimly Siegfried heard Mime's complaints and corrections and offers of help. But his patience had snapped forever. 'You could never weld the sword, so don't meddle now. I don't need the pap you call solder. I don't need your toothless rasp. I need splintered steel. I need the tree I felled in the forest to change into coal, I need the coal to glow, I need the glow to smelt the molten steel.'

Mime sensed, beyond any mortal or immortal question, that the sword would be forged, that Fafner would be slain, that the Ring and the Tarnhelm and the treasure would be Siegfried's. But the whole purpose of his life was that all this should be his. How could he be rid of Siegfried? He could brew a potion so powerful that one sip would make a man unconscious and a defenceless victim of his own sword. And Siegfried, exhausted from his battle with Fafner, would need the drink.

Siegfried, even in the heat of his heroical forging, noticed the dwarf at his sinister cookery. Mime cringed, admitted, evaded. But Siegfried forged on and the fire grew brighter, the molten steel glowed more magically, and the sparks flew higher and more prophetically, out of the humble cave.

Siegfried sang at his work, but Mime sat locked in a malevolent dream of Siegfried slaughtered, Alberich enslaved, and the whole race of the Nibelungs gripped by the power of Mime and his new-found dominion.

But the forge had become so hot, and the hammer blows so powerful, and the sword so tremblingly close to its birth, that all things else simply vanished into steam. Suddenly Siegfried gripped the red-hot, new-minted sword and plunged it into a great cold font of water. The steam made a cloud so huge it threatened to engulf heaven and earth and Nibelheim. But it cleared, and there in the little cave, set amidst endless miles of forest, stood Siegfried. And in his hand was the most powerful, the sharpest, the heaviest, and the brightest sword ever seen. It was Nothung. 'Look' said Siegfried. And he brought the sword down onto Mime's anvil in one huge sweep. The anvil split like an apple.

Confrontation of Wotan and Alberich

The world had caverns aplenty, and caves and caves and chasms and clefts and chinks in the armour of the earth.

In one of them, high on the topmost mountain of the gods' kingdom, slept Brünnhilde, finest and fieriest of the Valkyries, beloved of Wotan but disowned by him and set in a ring of terrifying flames to await the hero worthy of her. In another cave, far below in the forest, stood the shattered anvil of Mime, the dwarf Nibelung smith, who had abandoned his forest dwelling to accompany young Siegfried on his first journey into the world. But in the deepest and darkest corner of them all – Neidhöle – sat Fafner, the dragon. Behind him, in the depths of the cave, lay a gigantic hoard of gold. Enough to pledge and buy and redeem the world many times over. And amongst this treasure were two quite special objects: the Tarnhelm, which gave its wearer infinite choice of human or animal shape; and the Ring, which gave its bearer infinite power over the whole world.

One day, Fafner knew, someone would try to steal the gold. And that person might have special and magical powers. And that day was at hand. Witness the traffic of ruthless and ambitious characters prowling and skulking around the mouth of his cave. Alberich for one, dreaming of a new empire, but subject to the same panic-stricken fantasies as his evil brother, Mime, of how Fafner might surprise him. But the sounds he heard were not those of a dragon but of his most feared and hated enemy. Licht-Alberich was another name for Wotan, king of the gods. Schwarz-Alberich was the only and eternal name for the most evil of all the creatures of the underworld. Light and dark, black and white, the enmity was eternal.

And here, alongside Alberich in the deceptively beautiful glade outside Neidhöle, stood the Wanderer. But in spite of his eye patch, his long staff, his cloak and his wide-brimmed hat, the Wanderer was known to Alberich in a flash. He was Wotan.

At once the old hates and jealousies ignited. Each accused the other of the worst possible motives and intentions. Alberich warned Wotan that after his theft of the gold from Nibelheim and his payment of it to the Giants for building Valhalla, the runes he had carved into his spear would explode and consume him if he ever again tried to lay hands on the Rhine gold. Wotan had scarcely time to remind him that he knew his own runes well enough and that none of them bound him to Alberich, before Alberich raved again, caught in his obsessional dream of empire. He prophesied that since his curse had doomed anyone who owned the Ring, it would one day fall again to the Nibelungs (and that was always Wotan's nightmare). Because he, Alberich, wiser now and wiser always than those stupid Giants, would so deploy the power of the Ring that he would storm the ramparts of Valhalla and overwhelm its heroes with his legions of hell.

But Wotan had known Alberich's dark intentions long enough, and was in no way troubled by them. 'Who wins the Ring, wields it,' he proclaimed. Alberich knew Wotan of old, and he knew that Wotan relied always on the heroes he had sired to fulfil his great designs. Had he sired a new one, who should steal what he, Wotan, dared not touch? Wotan told him plainly that it was Alberich's own brother Mime who had reared a boy, specially trained and armed, who would kill Fafner for him. And neither Mime nor the boy even knew of Wotan's part in the quarrel. Alberich should look to his own. Alberich could not believe that Wotan would not join battle for the Ring, would not wade in to defend his own progeny.

'Heroes,' said Wotan, 'are my only answer to the world's woes. And they answer only to themselves. A hero will seize the Ring. Fafner, who guards it, will be slain. Two Nibelungs covet it. What will be the outcome? You want to know? I'll wake Fafner, so you can warn him of his death. Perhaps he'll give you the Ring?' And Wotan boldly called into the Neidhöle cavern to rouse Fafner from his sleep. And indeed Fafner awoke and roared. Alberich, unsettled as he was by Wotan's indifference, nevertheless followed his advice. He warned Fafner of his impending death at the hands of an all-conquering boy, but said that the boy's ambition centred only on the Ring. 'Give me the Ring, now,' wheedled Alberich, 'and I will make sure that you live and sleep and guard your treasure for ever.'

There was a silence, like a yawn. And then a crackle, like a fire being lit. 'I've got it, I'm keeping it. Let me sleep.' and the fire went out. Wotan laughed – that laugh that echoed around every corner of the forest and which no one ever forgot. 'No use Alberich,' he cried as he mounted his eight-winged steed. 'The trick didn't work. And nothing will work that is not true to its own nature. Watch your brother!'

Alberich, half astonished at the honesty of Wotan and half consumed with hate for him, watched, seething with envy, as the great war horse soared away from Fafner's cave. 'Laugh on,' said Alberich. 'Do you think I am mocked? Humiliated? I shall be a watcher at your funeral. Meantime, I shall watch here.'

At the entrance to the Neidhöle cave a sudden shaft of sunlight revealed two small and lonely figures: Siegfried and Mime. 'Here we are at last,' said Mime. 'And here we stay.'

'So here,' said Siegfried, 'is where I learn fear? Because if I don't, I shall go on alone and be rid of you at last.'

'My dear boy,' said Mime, 'if this place does not teach you fear then nothing will.' And he proceeded to give Siegfried the most frightening account of the dragon Fafner that he could imagine. (With his imagination he had often frightened himself half to death). How huge and savage he was, how wide his terrible jaws. How he swallowed people whole. How even the spray of his evil spittle shrivelled up both flesh and bone. How his snake-like tail, thrashing around him, would entwine innocent creatures and shatter them to fragments like glass.

Siegfried was amused, but not shaken. He recommended watching the dragon closely, avoiding it on its poisonous forays, but did not believe that he was in real danger. 'Perhaps I should shut his mouth for him?' was his first thought. But he asked one vital question: 'Does the dragon have a heart, and is it placed in the same part of him as it is in the rest of us?' On learning that it was, he asked whether plunging Nothung into that heart would count as knowing fear?

Mime told him that if the descriptions seemed tame, Siegfried had only to see the real thing and feel the ground tremble beneath its tread, then he would thank Mime for his trouble and realise how much Mime loved him.

Siegfried exploded with pent-up anger and disgust. 'I forbid you to love me. I've told you so often. Out of my sight! Leave me alone! I can't stand it any more!'

When, he wondered, could he finally be rid of this dwarf and his sickening nodding and blinking love!

Mime willingly withdrew. 'I'll go and rest by the spring. You stay here. When the sun is at its height, watch for the dragon: then he comes down to the stream to drink.'

But Siegfried called him back. 'If you and the dragon are at the stream, I'll let him pass. When he has drunk you up, then I'll stick him in his kidneys! If I were you I wouldn't rest by the spring. I would go as far away, as far away from me, as you can.'

But Mime could not resist the idea of his own cunning. How was he to know that his brother, and the all-seeing Wotan and even the innocent Siegfried, had long ago seen through it? 'After such a terrible fight, you will need me to refresh you. But call me if you need me or if, suddenly, you are afraid!' Mime sidled off into the forest. And the black, secret hope in his heart was that Fafner and Siegfried would fight the fearsome and long-awaited battle, and that neither would survive it. The dragon and the hero – both slain.

Siegfried stretched out under a huge tree and thought how happy he was that Mime was not his father. Mime's son, if he had one, would look like him, grey and old and dirty and hump-backed and lame and lop-eared and watery-eyed. What must Siegfried's father have been like? Like Siegfried he supposed. But his mother…? She must have been beautiful, surely, like the does of the forest. But why did she have to die? Did all human mothers die in childbirth? That surely would be too tragic. If only he could see, could have seen, his mother…

As Siegfried's regrets and daydreams seemed to merge with the murmuring of the forest, he began to hear, with almost unnatural clarity, the song of one particular bird in the woods. It seemed to be speaking to him, perhaps about his mother. That tiresome dwarf had once said he would one day understand the twittering of small birds. Perhaps it was possible? To encourage the bird he cut a reed with his sword and made a pipe of it. But the pipe wouldn't echo the bird, couldn't attract it. Siegfried threw it away and tried his horn. He was always trying to make friends by playing his horn. Up to now the only friends he had made were wolves and bears. Perhaps today he would have better luck. Perhaps the wood bird…? He put the horn to his lips and blew.

Siegfried slays Fafner the dragon

This horn call produced something so astonishing that Siegfried laughed aloud. 'Now I've found something really appealing. You could be the perfect companion I'm seeking.' What he had awoken was Fafner, yawning mightily in the entrance of his cave. Fafner could scarcely believe that anyone could stand so breezily in his cave mouth. 'What is this thing?' he growled. 'This thing needs to know fear,' said Siegfried, 'can you teach it to me?' 'How dare you?' roared Fafner. 'How I dare, I know not' replied Siegfried. 'But either you must teach me fear, or you must die.'

Fafner shuddered with fury. 'I was only looking for drink,' he growled, 'but now I have found dinner.' His dreadful maw opened, his rows of teeth shone, his spittle hissed and his breath burst into tongues of flame.

Fafner raged, Siegfried mocked and the woodland glade glowed orange with the fire and the heat. Trees shrivelled as the dragon's breath scorched them, and snapped in two as his great tail lashed them. Siegfried simply waited in the centre of this firestorm and then, with a sudden ringing cry, plunged his sword up to hilt into Fafner's black heart. The dragon uttered a huge, terrible gasp. 'Nothung lies in your heart,' said Siegfried calmly.

'Who roused you to this fight?' asked Fafner in a tired and old voice. No flames of defiance now, just resignation. 'You never sought it yourself.' 'I know so little,' said Siegfried, 'but it was you yourself who roused me to battle.'

'Ah,' said Fafner. 'Then let me tell you whom it is you have just murdered. I am Fafner, the last of the Giants. My brother Fasolt I slew, because of that deep-cursed Gold, used by the gods as payment to us. And you, young and rose-tinted like the dawn, have duly slain me. And the one who drove you to do it is now getting ready to slay you. Where do you come from?'

'My name is Siegfried' said the boy. 'But you can tell me where I come from, you with your ancient wisdom.'

But the dragon's ancient wisdom and his huge strength had ebbed away. 'Siegfried,' he intoned as if bewitched. And died. Siegfried, still no wiser about his parentage, pulled Nothung, his sword, out of the gigantic carcass. Blood spurted onto his hand. It stung. He licked his hand. 'This blood burns like fire,' he exclaimed. All around him the forest seemed to brood.

Siegfried has the Ring and the Tarnhelm

Suddenly to Siegfried it seemed full of voices. Not just the familiar calls and cries, but speaking voices, human voices even. Could that friendly wood bird be talking to him at last? Could that sip of dragon's blood be a kind of blessing?

Indeed the wood bird seemed to tell to him, as clear as could be, that Siegfried would own the Nibelung's treasures in the cave. And of course the Tarnhelm, which would cause him to undergo the most incredible adventures. Not to mention the Ring, which would quite simply make him the ruler of the world.

'Thank you,' said Siegfried, and walked into the cave.

No sooner had he stepped inside than Mime appeared, still in a state of terror. He was on the brink of conquering his fear and entering the dragon's lair, when his brother Alberich appeared, barring his way.

The blazing, unnatural hatred of the two dwarfs erupted yet again. Alberich accused Mime of plotting to gain a treasure that he never had the courage to steal. Mime accused Alberich of wielding a magic power that he never had the skill to fashion. Both knew that only Siegfried could resolve the struggle for the Ring. Mime had brought Siegfried up, but Alberich had Mime in his power. Mime bargained. Alberich laughed. Mime screamed with humiliation and spite. And suddenly Siegfried appeared, strolling out of the cavern's mouth with the Tarnhelm in one hand and the Ring in the other. Both Alberich and Mime were dismayed that the treasures they coveted most were those that Siegfried happened to have picked up. But the sight also sharpened their hatred for each other. And their greed. They slipped away into the forest to watch.

Siegfried cheerfully slipped the Ring onto his finger and the Tarnhelm onto his belt. 'I don't know what use they are,' he said to himself. 'Perhaps they're just reminders of the day's adventures, reminders that I slew Fafner the dragon and still never learned what fear was.'

Overhead his friendly wood bird seemed almost to hear these private thoughts. 'So Siegfried now owns the Ring and the Tarnhelm. But he shouldn't trust the treacherous Mime. He should listen very carefully. Then, because he has tasted dragon's blood, he will hear, behind all the hypocritical gush, what Mime really means to do.'

Siegfried stood, leaning on his sword. He smiled at the wood bird as she darted by. They understood each other. And he waited for Mime. Sure enough Mime was there, in the undergrowth, wondering why Siegfried was looking so carefully at the Ring and the Tarnhelm. Weighing up their value, he concluded, forgetting that Siegfried was not only unacquainted with fear but unacquainted with greed. Mime, always prey to the slightest suspicion, wondered whether a wanderer, wise and wily, might have wrought upon the boy. 'Runes,' he muttered to himself, 'I must be clever.'

But to Siegfried himself he was nothing but solicitude. Had he learned to fear? No? Had he slain the dragon? Yes? And was it very evil? Yes? Suddenly Siegfried shouted that there were more evil things alive than Fafner. More hated than the dragon he had slain was the creature that had driven him to it.

Mime was all conciliation, all understanding. 'You won't be seeing me much longer,' he whined. 'You won't be seeing anything much longer,' heard Siegfried. 'Now you have done the only deed I trained you for. All I need is to steal your booty. Easy to steal from a dumb innocent.'

Siegfried turned on Mime. 'You mean to hurt me?'

Mime was aghast. 'How could you think I said such a thing?' But something inside him knew that he had said it. He must be careful. So he picked his words very carefully. 'I have always had for you and your kin a special liking,' and Siegfried heard, clear as a bell, 'loathing'. 'I brought you up for one thing only. To win Fafner's Gold. Now you've done it, hadn't you better give me your life?' Siegfried grimly echoed the words. 'I never said that,' shrilled Mime. But he knew he had just thought it.

'You must be exhausted,' said Mime. 'Well, whilst you were forging your great sword, I was making a great brew. Drink it down and I'll have the sword and all the Gold.' Siegfried again echoed Mime's words and his obvious plan to rob Siegfried. Mime was aghast that his blackest and bitterest thoughts could appear as clear as daylight in even his cleverest speeches.

Mime made his most desperate attempt to appear normal and cool. 'You can't understand me at all. You misunderstand me at every chance. I take great pains to conceal my secret thoughts and reveal them only in impenetrable disguise yet you, stupid boy, blab them as if I had said them. Let me try once more. You have always liked my drinks. You always accepted them churlishly, but you always drank them.' Siegfried knew he badly needed some sort of refreshment. Even so, he asked how Mime had brewed this one. But Mime just said to trust him and drink the drink. And was somehow constrained to add, 'and your senses will soon sink into foggy oblivion. Then I could just steal the Gold and run. But if you ever awoke, I should never be safe from you. So best use your own sharp sword to hack your head off first.'

Siegfried understood immediately. This hatred of Mime seemed suddenly to be so natural and so well deserved. Mime roused himself to one last great effort of hypocrisy. 'No, no, you misunderstood. All I want is...' And suddenly disaster overcame all Mime's deceptions. 'All I want is...you out of my way. It's not just hate: it's revenge for all my humiliations; it's spite towards Alberich; it's my own way to the Gold. So drink. And you will never drink again!'

Siegfried had heard enough. Nothung the sword flashed once. Mime was dead in an instant. Siegfried scarcely gave him a look. No remorse, no regrets. Just silence, but a silence filled with the mirthless shudder of his brother, Alberich's, laughter.

Siegfried threw Mime's corpse onto the huge pile of Gold in the cavern and observed that it was Mime's deepest desire to be exactly there. 'And for a watchman,' he said, lugging the huge body of Fafner into the mouth of the cave, 'you will be safe from thieves.'

All at once, the heat of the day, the huge struggle he had undergone and the tangle of the forest's undergrowth were too much for Siegfried. He needed comfort and he needed help. It was to his new friend the wood bird that he confided all his woes: his mother's death, his father's death, his absolute dependence on a loathsome dwarf, his eternal loneliness...

The wood bird told Siegfried of a wondrous woman, asleep on a high rock, and of the terrifying fire surrounding her. Only to be awakened by a true hero. Siegfried was, himself, already on fire. His exhaustion was over and he was on his feet, pulsing with the splendour of the forest and the inspiration he breathed in from the wood bird. 'Can I, shall I, break through this fire?' he asked. And his little

wood bird piped that only someone who never felt fear could ever reach the sacred rock. 'That simple soul am I,' shouted Siegfried. 'But how shall I find her and her fiery rock? He looked up towards his wood bird and knew on the instant, that wherever she might soar, he must climb. And together they soared and they clambered up towards the fire-lit mountain where Brünnhilde, deep in her enchanted sleep, waited for her saviour, her awakener, her hero.

At the cleft foot of a very different mountain stood Wotan now – spear still in hand, but no longer gazing up to the heights where Loge absently watched over the defences of his beloved but abandoned daughter. Now he stood bellowing into the swirling fumes, which gushed unceasingly from a gigantic fissure in the surface of the earth. He was calling to Erda, wisest of all beings, the all-knowing Earth Mother. Calling her from her sleep in the deepest, fog-filled caverns of the earth to the bright daylight of the mountain heights. So Wotan sang his waking song, and an eerie blue light began to flicker. Out of the cleft appeared, as if carried, a figure out of ice and sparking with frost. Erda, still half frozen in sleep, knew well enough the power of the summons, felt deeply enough the compulsion of the spell.

'Who is it,' asked Erda, 'who draws me so irresistibly from my dreams of the future?'

'It is I' replied Wotan, and it is my wisdom which can command your awakening. And that wisdom I have won by wandering far and wide in the world. But no matter how far I travel, no one can share your vision. Where life is, there you breathe. Where thought is, there is your mind. What is hidden in the deepest

Wotan and Erda

depths is no secret to you. You are the height of every hill, the depth of every valley. You are in every drop of water, in every breath of air. All men say that you know all things, and therefore do I wake you.'

But Erda replied, 'I only sleep to dream, I only dream to think, I only think to work my wisdom. But the Norns do not sleep, they spin the rope of the world's destiny. And what they spin is my wisdom. Ask the Norns.'

Wotan said, 'The Norns are forever in bondage. As the earth spins, so they spin. They cannot change even the tiniest comma of history. From you I need to know how to stop the wheel of history in its tracks.'

Erda began to be troubled. 'The doings of men are always clouding my vision. Once a spirit even more powerful than mine possessed me. To Wotan I bore a child, a wish maiden who would choose him heroes from the battlefield. She is brave, she is wise. Ask her.'

Wotan told her of Brünnhilde's defiance, and of her punishment, but Erda grew even more disturbed. 'Ever since you woke me,' she cried, 'I have been troubled. Do you tell me that the Valkyrie, my child, has been punished with a sleep, whilst her mother slept? That you, the great teacher of defiance, has found defiance and punished it? That he who wills these happenings has seen them and been angry? That he who upheld justice, now rules by injustice? Let me go. My wisdom needs my sleep.'

But Wotan would not. 'It was you, Earth Mother, who first struck this god's bold heart with the sting of care. It was your ancient knowledge that wracked his spirit with fears of some dreadful, final calamity. Tell me then, wisest of the wise, how may this god conquer his own foreboding?'

'You are not what you say you are! What you are is wildness and stubbornness. Why have you broken my sleep?'

'You are not what you think you are! That primal earth wisdom of yours is at an end. All that you know dissolves in the face of my will. Do you know what Wotan wills? No, because your knowledge is no more. I will whisper it in your ear, so that you can return to your sleep untroubled. And now your sleep will be eternal. No longer do I agonise over the downfall of the gods. Now it has become my will. What once was a despairing resolve, made in an agony of conflict, I now perform in freedom and joy. I once vowed to leave the world to the greed of the Nibelungs; now I leave it to the noblest of the Volsungs. My chosen heir has never seen me, never heard a word of advice from me. Yet this valiant boy has won the Ring of the Nibelung. Radiant with love, unblackened by envy, and impervious to fear, he reduces Alberich's curse to impotence. And this is the hero destined to awaken Brünnhilde whom you bore to me. And your child of wisdom will one day perform a deed, which will redeem the whole world. So sleep now your everlasting sleep and you will see my end in your dreams. Know that whatever the future holds is joyfully bequeathed by an old god to his eternal youth. Down then, Erda, to your cavern. Down Earth Mother, mother of care, mother of fear. Down!'

And Erda half sank, half dissolved into her fathomless smoking pit. The eerie blue light of her ice cavern faded and in its place came the first rays of the sun. The earth seemed to come alive again, and

Siegfried destroys Wotan's spear

striding through the dawn came Siegfried, the wood bird still flying over him. Wotan stood quite still in the shadow of the rock, but the wood bird suddenly fluttered with alarm and flew off.

Siegfried was sad to see his companion and guide leave him so suddenly, but resolved to find the mountain himself. But suddenly he heard the voice of Wotan asking him where he was going. As soon as Siegfried told him of his quest for the burning mountain, Wotan wanted to know who had told him of it. As soon as Siegfried told of the wood bird, Wotan wanted to know how he could understand it, and then about the dragon he had killed, and the treacherous dwarf, and the sword, and the fragments from which he forged it, and who had made the fragments. Siegfried answered with growing impatience. How could he know who had made the fragments? And why wouldn't this old man tell him the way to the mountain? And when Wotan laughed, his temper finally snapped. 'If you can't tell me the way, then hold your tongue.' Wotan told him to be patient, to respect his years. Siegfried simply grew angrier. 'All my life an old man has stood in my way. Now I have swept him away. If you stand there much longer you may end up like Mime.' Then Siegfried strode over to him and inspected him closely and fearlessly – hat, cloak, one eye and all. 'You must have lost one eye to someone whose way you barred just too long. Mind you don't lose the other one now.'

Now Wotan began to feel offence. To be so insulted by the person he loved most in the world! But the more Wotan hinted at his powers and the dread that the Volsungs had once felt before him, the more contemptuous Siegfried

became. He was concerned only to reach the mountain the wood bird told him of. Wotan finally told him that the wood bird had left because it sensed the presence of the ravens and their master. Woe to that wood bird if the ravens ever caught it. 'The path it showed you is forbidden,' said Wotan, in real anger.

'And who are you to forbid me?' shouted Siegfried, now deeply roused.

'Beware the Guardian of the Rock,' said Wotan. 'It is I who keep the sleeping maiden prisoner, for if anyone should wake her, my power would vanish forever.' And he described how terrifying the fire would be. The graphic description had no more effect on Siegfried than had Mime's evocation of Fafner the dragon. He merely spurned Wotan and strode ahead towards Brünnhilde and the burning mountain. Finally Wotan was forced to bar the way with his spear and, in his anger, revealed that it was the same weapon that had once shattered Siegfried's sword into pieces. Siegfried instantly blazed with joy. He had found at last his father's enemy. Wotan thrust his spear forward. Siegfried whirled Nothung the sword once only and the great spear of the gods, carved with all the runes and treaties of the world's history, was hewn in two.

Siegfried climbs to the ring of fire

A long ominous roll of thunder sounded as the father of the gods picked up the broken fragments of the spear and vanished into the shadows. Siegfried heard only his voice: 'onwards, then. I cannot hold you longer.'

'A coward with a broken weapon,' shouted Siegfried contemptuously. And as he turned back to the path, suddenly the top of the mountain started to glow with fire and the flames seemed to stream downwards towards him. Overjoyed to find the fire which would lead him to his promised bride, Siegfried plunged into the flames, sheathing his sword, but blowing his horn. As his horn's call rang through the firestorm, he cried out, as so often before, for his heart's companion.

Fearless as ever, he defied what the gods and the earth might throw against him, and strangely, his very defiance seemed to make the flames paler and less threatening. As he strode up the mountain and his horn call rang off the glowing rocks, the fire swirled and flickered ahead of him and formed itself into an all-encompassing cloud, at first red as the angry flames which gave rise to it, and then gradually rosy as the dawn which was now breaking over the mountain tops and revealing, in the same enchanted stillness, the figures of the armoured Brünnhilde and her warhorse Grane, just as Wotan had left them countless years ago. As the flames finally died, and the stillness of the dawn reigned supreme, the figure of Siegfried could be seen, quite untouched by the fire but awed by the splendour of the scene which greeted him.

Siegfried comes upon Brünnhilde and Grane

He saw the war horse and wondered at the depth of its sleep, but then caught sight of the armoured figure. The sheer nobility of the creature made him wonder if he were not still dizzy from the flames he had defied. He drew off the helmet, less it should press too hard onto his hero's brow. He cut the thongs off the breastplate, lest it should circle too tightly this hero's breast. The golden hair fell free, and the body shivered and breathed anew. And Siegfried knew for the first time what love meant. And what fear meant. This extraordinary rapture made him gasp out a prayer to the only being of whom he had no real conception, but who he thought might offer some comfort and counsel – his mother.

Into the silence of Siegfried's new passion came no voice of counsel, only the pounding of his own heart. He knew well enough that somehow fear had come upon him. He was frightened, frightened to act, to speak, to do what he knew he must – awaken this radiant creature. In desperation, but also in passion, he placed a long, deep kiss on Brünnhilde's lips. And Brünnhilde awoke from her exile, with no bitterness, only wonder. She greeted the sun, the light, the day. Then she called to know who it was, what hero had awakened her from her enchanted sleep.

As soon as she heard Siegfried's name she greeted the shining earth and its gods. Her exaltation, and Siegfried's sudden ecstasy at the vision of power and beauty he had brought to life, seemed to feed on each other. Together they blessed the mother who had given birth to Siegfried, and the earth which had nourished him. Brünnhilde poured out to him the extent of her love for him, her ceaseless care for him even before he was born. Siegfried

wondered therefore if his mother were perhaps not dead. Brünnhilde told him his mother would never return. 'I am now your own being. What you know not, that I know. For your sake. Yet my knowledge is only my love. And my love is age-old, because only through me was Wotan's will expressed. The thought I could not name, because it was never a thought but only a feeling, I fought for, I defended. I defied even him who conceived it. I became the atonement. I was bound in punishment, because the thought I could only feel but never think was my love for you.'

Siegfried understood not a word of this. He sensed an ancient and wonderful wisdom but had no means of grasping it. He could not even contemplate the past, when all his senses were overwhelmed with the present. But now, for the first time, he was anxious, even afraid. And Brünnhilde seemed to grow sad and pensive. Whilst Siegfried was burning with desire, thirsting for her lips, feeling the new wound in his heart, believing that the fire he had endured quite unharmed on the mountain now burned even more savagely inside him, Brünnhilde was beginning to have flashes of memory of her heroic past. Grane, who had slept away the ages with her, was now awake and browsing. Her shield and helmet were laid aside and unavailing. Her armour, cut from her body, was now quite unprotective.

The love scene: Siegfried and Brünnhilde

Siegfried embraced her, all impetuosity. But suddenly Brünnhilde tore herself away as if terrified. She recalled that not even the gods had desired her; every hero had been in awe of the virgin maid. Even as she was cast out of Valhalla she was sanctified. But now her breastplate was snapped. She was Brünnhilde no longer.

To Siegfried she was still the beautiful maiden sunk in a sleep from which it seemed he had still not awakened her. But she, frightened by the loss of her ancient wisdom, felt clouds gathering to shut out the light from her. And in that darkness she imagined horrors stalking her. She put her hands over her eyes in terror. Siegfried gently pulled them away, telling her that closed eyes only bring on the night. 'Open your eyes. Out of the darkness and into the sun-bright day.' But the sunlight only seemed to deepen Brünnhilde's sense of shame and pain. She begged Siegfried, her hero and the light and treasure of the earth not to touch her, not to violate her. Let him keep his love for himself.

But Siegfried had lost himself entirely in the wonder of his new passion. And the passion burned so scorchingly that all he could think of was to plunge into the cooling stream of Brünnhilde's love. His ardour aroused hers, until she feared lest he, at last, be himself afraid of the turbulence of this all-consuming woman. But fear was forgotten. The pair laughed in their new happiness. Brünnhilde called on the Norns to cut the ropes of fate and bring on the twilight of the gods, as herald of the bright day where she and her hero would live in bliss.

TWILIGHT OF THE GODS

(Götterdämmerung)

The Norns weaving the strands of destiny

utside the cave where Brünnhilde and Siegfried slept, on the very rocks to which the Valkyries had once flocked with their grim harvest of heroes killed in battle, three tall, veiled women sat in gloomy silence. They were the Norns, the all-knowing sisters whose task it was to spin the destiny of the world with the golden rope of knowledge. It was night, and the only light came from Loge's great circle of fire that blazed far below them. Knowing they must start to spin again, the Norns stretched the rope between a pine and the rocks around the cave. They sang as they wove, of the past and of the future, of history and destiny.

They sang of a great tree, the World Ash Tree, to which their rope had once been anchored. It grew in a magical glade, and beneath it welled up a spring, its streams whispering ancient wisdom. Wotan, mightiest of the gods, came there to drink at the spring. He had hewn a great branch from the tree, and it was from this branch that he made his mighty spear. Into its shaft he carved his runes, the unbreakable promises and treaties of the world. But the tree sickened of the wound that Wotan had inflicted. Its leaves turned yellow, it withered and died, and the spring beneath it dried up. The spear itself now lay in splinters, shattered by Siegfried's sword. On Wotan's orders, the slain heroes of Valhalla brought the withered branches of the World Ash Tree and piled them up around their castle's great hall.

'One day,' sang the third sister, spinning her golden rope, 'Wotan will plunge the splinters of the spear into Loge's heart, and a fire will spring up so fierce that it will ignite the branches piled round Wotan as he sits in his great hall. Valhalla will be consumed in the flames, and that will be the fiery end of the old gods.'

The Norns' eyes were clouded: they could see nothing but visions of calamity. The great golden rope of destiny began to slacken and to fray on the sharp edges of the rocks. Suddenly it snapped. The Norns, crying out in despair at the loss of their wisdom, snatched up the pieces and plunged back into the earth, back to their mother Erda.

Now the day dawned and Siegfried and Brünnhilde emerged from their cave. They were still radiant from their night together, but Siegfried was already driven on to seek new adventures. Brünnhilde did nothing to hold him back. She had only one regret – that everything she knew, and everything she was, she had already given to Siegfried; that she had nothing more to give. But Siegfried told her that she had given him more than he could ever fathom. What he did know, and wondered at, was the thought of her, ever-present in his mind.

'If you want to show your love for me,' she urged him, 'think of yourself and what you have achieved. Remember the fire you fearlessly strode across, remember the shield and the helmet you loosed to awaken me, and remember the eternal oaths we have sworn.'

Leaving Brünnhilde to the protection of the sacred ring of fire, Siegfried gave to her, as a pledge, the Ring. The Ring which the dragon Fafner had guarded for so long, and which Siegfried believed represented the sum of his achievements. In exchange Brünnhilde gave Siegfried her beloved horse Grane. She told him how Grane once flew aloft and bore her fearlessly through storms and lightning. But just as she had been deprived of her divine wisdom and strength, so had Grane lost the power of flight. Still, the horse would follow Siegfried fearlessly

Siegfried's Rhine journey

wherever he led. 'Take good care of him,' she begged, 'and he will understand what you say to him. But speak often of Brünnhilde.'

Siegfried vowed that he would accomplish his deeds of valour while inspired by Brünnhilde. *She* would choose his battles, and *hers* would be his victories. He was no longer Siegfried but the arm of Brünnhilde. 'Then we are one,' she cried, 'eternally one.'

Siegfried and Grane plunged down the mountain to the Rhine and the boat that awaited them. Far above, Brünnhilde watched as the vessel bearing her only-beloved hero grew smaller and smaller on the swirling waters of the Rhine. And the Rhine itself watched, as the future floated down the great stream of the past.

Siegfried and Grane watched, too, as the golden meadows and the dark forests drifted past. The cool clear call of Siegfried's horn echoed along the cool clear waters of the river. And very faintly it echoed into the dark but spacious hall of the Gibichungs' castle on the Rhine. There sat Gunther, Lord of the Gibichungs, and his beautiful sister Gutrune. But there too sat grim Hagen, his half-brother. His mother was Grunhilde, mother to Gunther and Gutrune – but it was the hateful Alberich who had fathered Hagen on her, and Hagen was as evil, as dangerous and as cunning as his father. He already knew the story of the Ring that had once belonged to Alberich, and was desperate to possess it for himself.

Hagen proclaimed his respect for his trueborn brother, and Gunther in turn praised Hagen's wise counsels. 'Are we not lords worthy of the fame of the Gibichungs?' asked Gunther. But Hagen replied that one thing was still wanting:

Gunther had no wife, and Gutrune no husband.

The Gibichungs asked Hagen where they might find a bride and a husband worthy enough to enhance the glory of their House. So Hagen told them the story of Siegfried and Brünnhilde and of the magic circle of fire, which only Siegfried could cross.

'But how,' asked Gunther, 'can I bring Brünnhilde home, when I can never cross the fire?'

'Siegfried would bring her to you if he were bound to your sister,' replied Hagen.

'You are wicked to mock me Hagen,' cried Gutrune. 'How can I win the greatest hero on the earth, when the loveliest woman has already won him?' Then Hagen reminded them of the dark, secret drink he had discovered and brought back to them. If Siegfried were to drink one draught of it he would forget Brünnhilde, forget that he had ever seen a woman, and be enslaved by Gutrune.

Brother and sister were delighted with this treacherous plan, but could not imagine how they would find Siegfried. And yet the echoes of his horn were floating down the Rhine toward them even as they plotted.

The Gibichung brother and sister, as Siegfried arrives at their hall

Hagen strode towards the huge gates that opened onto the river, as if he had foreseen this very moment. 'Hail Siegfried!' he cried, and sure enough there was the boat moored and Siegfried and Grane walking into the Gibichung courtyard.

'I come seeking Gibich's son,' cried Siegfried. 'To his very hall you are welcome,' replied Hagen.

'Which is he?' asked Siegfried. Gunther stood forth. 'Will you fight with me or be my friend?' asked Siegfried.

'Speak no more of fighting,' answered Gunther, 'you are welcome here.'

'Will you tend my horse?' asked Siegfried. 'There is no nobler steed in the world.' But as Grane was led gently away to his stable, Siegfried wondered. 'You called to me as Siegfried,' he said. 'Have you seen me before?'

Hagen replied at once. 'We knew you by your strength. The current was against you but you drove your boat up the river with one stroke of your oar.'

Gunther offered to Siegfried his land, his people and his allegiance. But in return Siegfried could only offer himself, and Nothung, the sword he had forged. Hagen quietly reminded him that he was believed to possess the Nibelungs' hoard of Gold. Siegfried told him that he thought so little of the Gold that he left it in the cave where Fafner had once guarded it.

'Did you take nothing?' asked Hagen.

'Oh, this piece of Gold net,' said Siegfried. 'But I have no idea of its purpose.'

But Hagen knew well enough. 'It is the Tarnhelm,' he said. 'Put it over your head and it will make you invisible, it will change your shape. It will transport you to the farthest ends of the earth in a moment, no matter how distant. But did you keep nothing else from that hoard of treasure?'

'Just a ring,' said Siegfried. Hagen, now as tense as a drawn bowstring, asked very carefully if he had it safe. 'It is in the keeping of a wondrous woman,' said Siegfried. Hagen knew then that the cursed ring he desired so much was with Brünnhilde.

Gunther, for his part, asked nothing of Siegfried. His sister came in with the magic drink and offered it sweetly to Siegfried, who accepted it with friendly courtesy. He raised the drinking-horn in a salute to Brünnhilde and, all unaware of the terrible irony of his words, said: 'If ever I forgot all you taught me, one thing would remain – the gift of true love.' Then he drained the horn in one great draught.

The effect was instantaneous. Siegfried rose to his feet and gazed into Gutrune's eyes, grasping her hand and offering himself to her. Gutrune looked back with mute submission.

'Gunther, have you a wife?' asked Siegfried. Gunther told him of the wonderful woman called Brünnhilde and how she was protected by a ring of fire that he was not allowed to pass. Not a flicker of recognition passed over Siegfried's face – to him it was a wondrous tale newly told. 'I fear no fire,' he cried. 'I will win your bride for you, if you will grant me your sister.'

The oath of blood brotherhood

'I will gladly grant you my sister,' said Gunther, 'but how will you win Brünnhilde for me when you are Siegfried?'

'I shall wear the Tarnhelm,' replied Siegfried. 'I shall become Gunther.'

'Then we must drink blood-brotherhood,' cried Gunther, seizing a drinking-horn and filling it with wine. The two pricked their arms and mixed their blood with the wine. Then, as Hagen held the horn between them, they swore the eternal oath and drank the wine.

'Hagen, why did you not join in the oath?' asked Siegfried.

'My blood would have spoiled the draught. It is not red and noble like yours, but cold and sluggish,' Hagen replied, so Siegfried split the drinking horn in two with one stroke of his sword Nothung.

Siegfried burned with desire to set out on his newest adventure. Gunther would spend the night on the boat whilst Siegfried climbed the mountain to Brünnhilde's cave. As they rushed to the river, Gutrune came out to ask Hagen why they were in such haste. 'They hasten to woo Brünnhilde. And Siegfried hastens to win you.' Gutrune smiled in wonder. 'Siegfried – mine!' she whispered.

Hagen was left to guard the hall, and as he sat there, spear in hand, he brooded in the darkness. Siegfried would bring home a bride for Gunther, but for Hagen he would bring home the Ring. 'You both think me so low born,' he whispered into the night, 'but you are my vassals. You serve the Nibelung!'

The despair in Valhalla

Brünnhilde sat at the entrance to her cave, dreaming of Siegfried, when she heard a distant roll of thunder and the sound of a rushing through the air. She knew it of old, one of the mighty Valkyrie horses flying through the storm. A distant voice called, 'Brünnhilde, do you still sleep, or are you awakened?' and she recognised the voice of her sister Waltraute.

'Waltraute,' she cried, 'you know the wood below. Tether your horse and come to me.' Brünnhilde rushed down to bring Waltraute to the mountain top. 'Are you not afraid?' she asked. 'How did you dare to defy Wotan and fly to me, or has his heart softened? He knew well enough when I defended Siegfried, that I fought for his dearest wish. And when he bound me to this rock, he girdled me with fire, so that only the finest of all heroes could win me. And so it was. I have found love and laughter. Have you come to share that bliss?'

Waltraute thought her sister's ecstasy a madness. Brünnhilde's courage in defying Wotan her sister likewise considered a danger so dire that she could not comprehend it. Waltraute told her bewildered sister of the deadly peril faced by Valhalla and the gods who ruled there. 'Ever since Wotan parted from you, he never once sent the Valkyries into battle, never once glanced at the ranks of heroes in his hall. Alone, he paced across the world, never sleeping, never resting. Then finally he came home. In his hands were the splinters of his sacred spear, shattered by the sword of a hero. He sent the warriors of Valhalla to the stricken World Ash Tree to cut it down and pile the logs in a mighty palisade around Valhalla. Then he called a Council of the Gods to sit beside him in the great hall, with the Valkyries and their heroes ranged around. There he still sits, silent as the grave, with his shattered spear in his hand. Freia's apples of eternal youth he eats no more. The gods too sit motionless, frozen with fear and foreboding. Once he sent his two ravens out into the world. If they returned with glad tidings from his domain, then the gods would smile again. But they never came back.

'We Valkyries lie clasping his knees, and once I threw myself weeping on his breast. Then his look softened, and he thought of you, Brünnhilde. As if in a dream he whispered, "If only she gave the Ring back to the Rhinemaidens, then the world and the eternal gods would be free of Alberich's curse." So I stole away through the silent ranks of Valhalla, mounted my horse, and rode through the storm to you. Now my sister, I beg you, do what is in your power alone; end the agony of the gods.'

Brünnhilde only half understood what Waltraute told her. Valhalla and the gods were scarcely a memory to her, like a swirling incomprehensible mist. 'What would you have me do?' she asked.

'That Ring on your finger,' said Waltraute, 'throw it away, into the Rhine. Give it back to the Rhinemaidens.'

Brünnhilde was outraged. Give the Ring, throw it away, when it was Siegfried's pledge of love? She thought that her sister must be mad. But Waltraute knew that all the troubles of the world, and all the despair of Wotan and the gods, stemmed from that Ring and the curse upon it. One act of sacrifice from Brünnhilde could end it.

Brünnhilde would not listen. 'Have you no conception, my unfeeling sister,' she stormed, 'of what bliss this Ring represents to me?' This Ring is Siegfried's

Gunther (Siegfried in disguise) and Brünnhilde

love for me. And that is more than Valhalla, more than Wotan, more than all the eternal gods. Go back and tell them that I will never forswear my great love, that they will never take it, and the Ring that pledges it, from Brünnhilde. Not even if Valhalla's glittering splendour should collapse in ruins. Quickly, mount your horse and tell them that!'

Waltraute rushed to her horse, and as it rose into the stormy air her voice could be heard crying 'Woe! Woe to you sister! And woe to the eternal gods,' until the thunder was only a mutter and the lightning only a flicker, leaving Brünnhilde alone in the gathering dusk.

But the glow from the girdle of fire below seemed suddenly to grow brighter. Tongues of flame shot up around the rocks. And from below came the unmistakable sound of Siegfried's horn. Brünnhilde was on her feet in an instant – 'Siegfried' she cried, 'Siegfried is back.' And she rushed to the edge of the rocky cliff to greet her hero. But it was a dark and sinister figure that leapt to the cliff-top beside her. Brünnhilde screamed in terror, 'I am betrayed!'

Siegfried spoke with the voice of Gunther, whose shape he had already assumed. 'I come as a hero who fears no fire, and as a suitor who will have your hand in marriage.'

'Who are you that can pass the fire that consumes all but the strongest?'

'One who will master you, whether you will or not.'

'You are some monster, some evil bird of prey come to destroy me,' gasped Brünnhilde. 'Are you a hideous legion of the night?'

'I am a Gibichung, and Gunther is my name. This is the name of the man that must be yours.'

Brünnhilde turned to the dark sky where Waltraute had vanished and whispered, 'Wotan, you merciless god, you merciless father, now at last I understand my punishment. Not just misery, but mockery.'

The figure advanced on her. 'Night draws on. Into the cave. There you shall be wedded to me.'

Brünnhilde turned on him blazing, the Ring on her finger thrust out like a weapon. 'Keep back. This Ring is my power, this pledge is my protection, no force can compel me to shame whilst I hold its fearful power.'

Siegfried instantly wrenched it from her finger and said, 'It is with this Ring that you shall be wedded to Gunther. Brünnhilde, shattered and defeated, sank into the cave. Siegfried, before following, drew Nothung from its sheath, and said, in his own clear voice, 'Lie between us tonight, my sword, and bear witness of my loyalty to my brother Gunther.'

At night in the Gibichung hall, spear and shield by his side, Hagen slept. Into his sleep came the voice of his father Alberich.

'Are you asleep, Hagen my son? Do you hear me?'

'I hear you, Father,' said Hagen, still half asleep. 'What have you to tell me?'

'Remember the power that could be ours, if only you have the courage of your mother when she bore you to me?'

'I have my mother's courage but little I owe to you. I am pale and wan, old before my time. In my life there is no joy, and I hate those who possess it.' Alberich was content that his son should hate the happiness of others, but demanded that he love his joyless father as he should. And he told Hagen of the plight of Wotan and the gods and of their imminent doom.

Wotan was no longer a menace to them. 'Then who shall inherit the power of the gods?' asked Hagen.

'We shall,' whispered Alberich from his hiding place under the Gibichung hall. 'You and I, if I can trust you if you share my hatred and my fury. Siegfried now has the Ring. Both Valhalla and Nibelheim are in his power. But he knows nothing of that power, and my terrible curse has no hold over him. Innocent that he is, he burns his life away in laughter and love. Only the destruction of this hero can serve our turn. Do you hear me, Hagen, my son?'

'Even now,' said Hagen, 'and at my command, he hastens to his doom.'

'That golden Ring,' insisted Alberich, '*that* you must have. If it were ever returned to the Rhinemaidens who once tricked me, then it would be lost to us forever. So now, unceasingly, strive for the Ring. Stronger than any dragon, stronger than any hero, our hatred shall win the Ring. Swear it to me, Hagen my son.'

'I swear it to myself,' retorted Hagen. And Alberich disappeared, back to the dark, despairing vaults of Nibelheim.

Dawn broke over the Rhine and Hagen awoke from his troubled sleep. Suddenly, Siegfried materialised before him, looking for Gutrune. She came running, full of questions about the great adventure. So Siegfried told them of the night on Brünnhilde's rock and the magic of the Tarnhelm, of his own chastity and of the imminent arrival of Gunther and Brünnhilde. Hagen had seen their sail from far off. Gutrune called on him to summon the Gibichung vassals to welcome them to the wedding feast, and departed to summon the women.

So Hagen took up the huge steer horn at the door and blew it so that it carried across the fields and the river and the rocks. But his cry was the war cry, the signal of peril and alarm. 'Hoiho. Hoiho. Men of Gibich, to arms! Danger surrounds us! Bring your trustiest weapons! Hoiho!'

Soon the rocks were swarming with the Gibichung vassals, armed to the teeth, and shouting, 'We are here, Hagen, ready for battle. Who is the foe? Where is the danger? Is Gunther in peril? We are here to defend him!'

And Hagen shouted back 'Gunther has won himself a wife.'

And the vassals shouted, 'Is he pursued, are her angry kinsmen after his blood?'

'He comes alone, no enemy follows,' said Hagen.

The vassals, puzzled now, asked, 'Has he then overcome them, has he won the fight?'

'Siegfried the dragon killer kept him safe.' The vassals, more puzzled than ever, now wanted to know what they could do. What service could they give? Hagen told them to slaughter cattle for Wotan, a bear for Froh, a goat for Donner, and sheep for Fricka.

'And then,' asked the vassals, 'what must we do?'

'Take your drinking horns in your hands,' replied Hagen. 'Drink till you are awash with wine to make the gods smile on this marriage.' The vassals exploded into laughter. If even the grim Hagen could be so cheerful, they thought, then light and laughter really had come to the land. But Hagen soon silenced their laughter. 'Now greet Brünnhilde, bride of Gunther. She is your lady. Serve her with loyalty. And if ever she is wronged, avenge her swiftly.'

Gunther and Brünnhilde stepped into the hall, and the vassals sang the resounding age-old bridal greeting to them. Gunther presented Brünnhilde to them as the noblest wife that ever was won, a woman who would raise the race of the Gibichungs to its highest acclaim. Brünnhilde stood silent, her eyes cast down, never once looking up. Then he greeted the other bridal pair as they too stepped into the hall: his sister Gutrune and Siegfried.

At the sound of Siegfried's name, Brünnhilde suddenly looked up and was devastated to find him standing beside her on the arm of Gutrune. 'Siegfried, here?' she cried. 'Gutrune?' She staggered, on the point of fainting. The vassals were alarmed and Siegfried called to Gunther to support his wife.

'Brünnhilde,' he said 'open your eyes. There is your husband.' Brünnhilde dimly understood that Siegfried did not recognise her, but her ancient wisdom was far behind her now, and she could not fathom the plot that surrounded her.

Then she spied the Ring itself, glittering on Siegfried's finger. 'Ha!' she cried, 'that Ring!'

And her voice rang round the hall. The vassals were immediately on their guard, and Hagen was once again as grim and tense as ever. 'Listen well to this woman's appeal,' he counselled.

So Brünnhilde demanded of Siegfried how he got the Ring from Gunther, the Ring with which she was newly married to him. And Siegfried replied that he never had it from Gunther. And Gunther confirmed that he gave no Ring to Siegfried. 'Yet you know it well, Brünnhilde,' he said. Suddenly the truth, or some fragment of the truth dawned on Brünnhilde. She rounded on Siegfried.

'It was you, you thief, who wrenched the Ring from my finger!'

Siegfried in turn was outraged. 'That Ring I never won from woman, I won it as booty from the terrible fight at Neidhöle where I slew the dragon.'

But Hagen, cunning as ever, turned to Brünnhilde. 'You know that Ring well. If it is the Ring you gave to Gunther as a pledge of your betrothal, then it is Gunther's. Siegfried must have won it by fraud and treachery. And for that he must pay!'

'Treachery!' echoed Brünnhilde, 'treachery beyond all shame.'

The whole hall, and the army of vassals, were plunged into confusion. 'Treachery,' they shouted, 'treachery to whom?'

Brünnhilde, alone in her misery and confusion, glared up towards Valhalla and the gods. 'You decreed for me,' she cried in fury, 'such misery as none has ever known. Then teach me a vengeance such as none has ever known. Let me bring to his ruin the man who has betrayed me, with such an anger as may never be stilled!'

Gunther tried to calm her in vain. 'Away!' she hissed at him. 'You, the betrayer, are yourself betrayed. Know, all of you,' she called out to the echoing hall, 'that I am already wed, to Siegfried there.'

Amidst the instant turmoil and confusion in the hall, Siegfried's voice carried clearly. He in turn rounded on Brünnhilde. 'Have you so little care for your own honour? Must I be the one to give your slanders the lie? Let everyone here know this. To Gunther I swore blood-brotherhood, and my good sword Nothung lay between this woman and me to stand watch over my oath of loyalty.'

But Brünnhilde blazed forth again. 'You cunning, crafty hero. See how you lie. I know well enough the power of your

The oath of vengeance on Siegfried

sword. But in its sheath it lay whilst you made love to me.'

The tumult in the hall grew louder, the vassals clamouring to know if their lord Gunther had been wronged. Even Gunther and Gutrune seemed to have forgotten their complicity in the trick which had caused this uproar, and called, like the vassals, on Siegfried to swear an oath that would clear him of this terrible accusation.

In the silence which followed, Siegfried asked innocently, 'If I am to swear an oath, on whose weapon shall I swear it?'

On an instant, Hagen offered his spear, and the vassals crowded round in a ring. Siegfried laid his hand on the spear and swore a solemn oath. 'Let this steel pierce me, let this spear slay me, if this woman's words are true and I broke my oath to my brother.'

And then Brünnhilde strode into the circle, laid her own hands on the spear, and swore, 'Let this steel pierce him, let this spear slay him, for he has sworn an oath and it is a lie!'

The vassals called on Donner to send down thunder from on high and silence this shame to the house of Gibichung. But Siegfried, jubilant as ever, called to Gunther to look to his wild new wife, and wait till her fury, which some demon must have aroused, should calm itself. And he called to the vassals to follow him to the feast. 'Leave the squabbling of women,' he laughed, 'and join me in the joy of the wedding. Let the women join me too. Perhaps the Tarnhelm only half concealed me, and my plan was only half successful. I am as disappointed as any of you, but you shall find me as joyous as anyone at the feast. Come, share that joy with me,' and, seizing Gutrune's arm,

he processed into the banqueting hall with all the vassals and all the women following him.

Brünnhilde was left alone with Hagen and Gunther. She knew that she had been a victim of trickery and of evil. But all her wisdom had been taken from her, all her strength had passed to Siegfried. She belonged to him, his supreme gift. And yet he seemed blithely to give this gift away. She could not understand: the runes were no longer to be read. Whose sword, she wondered, would cut the bonds around her?

As if in answer to her thoughts, Hagen was behind her, whispering into her ear: 'Trust me. I am the one who will have vengeance on the man who betrayed you.'

But Brünnhilde turned on him in scorn. 'One glance from his eye would shrivel your brightest courage. Your spear will need more than perjury and the breaking of oaths if you are to overcome the mightiest of all heroes.'

So Hagen said, 'Then I need your secret counsel, If I am to avenge you.'

'My magic protects him,' said Brünnhilde. 'No weapon can slay him, except...'

'Except...?' asked Hagen, quick as a snake.

'Siegfried could never turn his back on any foe, any danger,' said Brünnhilde, 'so there my blessing and my magic are absent.'

'In his back then,' said Hagen, almost to himself, 'shall my spear strike.'

Then he turned to his half-brother, who was sunk in the deepest despair. 'Stand up Gunther, noble lord of the Gibichungs,' he cried. 'Here sits your noble wife. Why are you so hung about with grief?'

Siegfried will not return the Ring to the Rhinemaidens

But Gunther could do nothing but bewail his shame, his infamy. Brünnhilde poured scorn on him. 'You cowardly creature! Cowardly and false! You hid behind a hero, so that he should win for you the renown you could not win yourself. So low is your noble race sunken.'

Gunther writhed in shame. 'I am a deceiver, and I have been deceived. I am a traitor and I have been betrayed. My breast should be splintered and my bones crushed to dust! Help me, Hagen. Help me to save my honour.'

Hagen gave him one hope only.

'There is no skill of the hand, no trick of the mind, that can help you. Only one thing will serve,' he said. 'The death of Siegfried.'

Gunther was horrified. 'But we have sworn blood-brotherhood!'

'The bond is broken' replied Hagen, 'and the oath now calls for his blood.'

Gunther still did not understand how he had been deceived by Siegfried or how the bond had been broken. Brünnhilde, in her cold fury, told him that he had been betrayed by all of them. 'If I called down the retribution that is mine, all the blood in the world would not wash away your guilt. But the death of one will stand for all. Siegfried shall fall to atone for himself, and for all of you.'

Hagen was already at Gunther's ear, whispering, 'He shall fall, but for your good. The Ring he wears will bring you power beyond your dreams once he is dead.'

'Brünnhilde's Ring?'

'It is the Nibelung's Ring!'

Gunther still feared for his sister – how could they face her if they slew her husband? Brünnhilde raged against her as the sorceress who stole her husband, but Hagen, as always, had a scheme to hide their guilt. 'Tomorrow,' he said, 'there is a hunt. Perhaps Siegfried will be slain by a boar.'

So each of them had powerful reasons to contrive the death of Siegfried, and the three swore a solemn oath of vengeance upon him, just before the doors of the hall burst open and the happy throng, with Siegfried and Gutrune in its midst, came streaming in.

Next morning the hunt was on. Gunther and Hagen and Siegfried and all the Gibichung vassals swarmed across the fields and woods and mountains beside the Rhine. Hunting spears gleamed everywhere, and the sound of horns echoed from every valley and cleft. Below, in the Rhine itself, the three Rhinemaidens swam around in a playful circle, rejoicing in the sunshine, but always recalling the days when its rays shone upon their treasure, the gold of the Rhine, long since stolen from them. They called on the sun to send them the hero who would give them back their gold. And as if in answer came the sound of Siegfried's horn, ringing across the river. He was in hot pursuit of a bear who had mysteriously disappeared.

'Some elf has tricked me,' he said to himself in good humour. 'Where have you hidden my quarry?' And then, coming suddenly to the river, he spied the Rhinemaidens in all their shimmering silvery beauty.

'Siegfried,' they chorused, 'what elf is this, that has led you so far astray? Tell us about him.'

'Aha,' laughed Siegfried, 'is it you who have lured away my bear? Do you have him in your lair? Is he your sweetheart?'

'What would you give us Siegfried,' asked the Rhinemaidens, 'if we gave you back your hunting prize?'

'He will be my only trophy in this hunt,' said Siegfried cheerfully, 'so ask what you will.'

'There is a gold Ring glittering on your finger,' said the maidens. 'Why not give us that?'

'To win that Ring,' said Siegfried, 'I slew a dragon. Are you asking me to give it up for a bearskin?'

'So mean, so niggardly, so beggarly,' mocked the Rhinemaidens. 'Where is your generosity to women?'

'If I wasted my wealth on you,' replied Siegfried, 'my wife would be furious.'

The girls dissolved into laughter. 'Oh, she must be a harpy! Does she beat you? Yes, our hero can already feel her hand smacking him!'

'Laugh away,' said Siegfried. 'Teasing will never get you this Ring.' The Rhinemaidens plunged back into the river and Siegfried caught their distant mockery: 'So strong, so handsome, but so mean, so miserly! What a shame.'

Siegfried, left alone, asked himself why he bothered with their teasing, half praise and half mockery. Maybe he should have given them the Ring? 'Come back,' he called into the Rhine, 'and I'll give you the Ring.' He drew it from his finger, ready. The Rhinemaidens soared up to him from the depths of the river, but now they were no longer the playful, seductive creatures they had been a moment ago. Now they were solemn, even grim. 'Guard the ring well until you understand all the misfortune that it holds. Then you will be grateful if we free you from its curse.'

Siegfried put the Ring back on his finger. 'Tell me what you know of it,' he said.

'We know of evil coming towards you. That Ring you hold is your own doom. It is made of the stolen gold of the Rhine,

and the creature who cunningly forged it, when he lost it to another, laid a terrible curse on it. The curse brings death upon whoever wears it. This very day it will bring death to you just as you brought death to the dragon, unless you surrender the ring to us so we may bury it deep in the Rhine. Only the waters of that eternal river can wash away the curse.'

Siegfried was scornful. 'You cunning creatures,' he smiled. 'I was not taken in by your flattery. I am even less taken in by your threats.'

'Believe us, Siegfried!' cried the Rhinemaidens desperately. 'We tell you the truth. The curse was woven by the Norns into the never-ceasing golden rope of fate.'

Proud as ever, Siegfried answered them: 'My sword once splintered a huge spear. No matter how deep into the eternal rope the curse may be woven, Nothung will slice the rope like a hair. The dragon warned me of the curse, but he never frightened me. If a Ring like this were to make me master of the whole world, I would give it away in a moment as a token of love. But under a threat, I would never yield it. Not even if it were worth less than a snap of the fingers. And as for my life…' He paused, and picked up a lump of clay at his feet. 'Look, I throw it behind me!'

The Rhinemaidens despaired of him and dived down into the Rhine again.

But as they dived they knew his fate. 'So wise and so strong, he thinks himself,' they said to each other, 'though he is blind, and bound hand and foot. He does not know that the oaths that he swore are forsworn. He does not know that the runes he received, he cannot read. He does not know that he has spurned the great gift he received. All he has is the Ring that will bring him his death. But today it will come to a wondrous woman, and she will understand us better than him.'

Siegfried only heard the distant murmur of their prophecy as he sat beside the river. 'Now I know', he said, 'that in water, as on land, the ways of women are the same. They tempt you – you reject them. They threaten you – you repulse them. And then they berate you! All the same, if I were not so true to Gutrune, one of those ravishing Rhinemaidens…'

Suddenly the hills and rocks above were alive with the horn calls of the Gibichungs. Siegfried answered with his own.

'At last we have found you,' said Hagen.

'Come down, it's cool here by the river,' said Siegfried.

So Hagen called a halt to the hunt as the vassals climbed down to the river. 'Here we will share our spoils and pass round the wine.'

Siegfried confessed that he had caught nothing. 'I went after a bear,' he said, 'but all I found were water fowl. If I had been better provided for the hunt, I might have brought back three water creatures who told me I should be slain – there on the Rhine!'

'A bad day's hunting, if the hunter himself were slain by some lurking beast,' said Hagen, joining in the general laughter.

Siegfried was thirsty and called for wine. Hagen offered him a drinking horn and asked, 'Is it true, as they say, Siegfried, that you can understand the song of birds?'

Siegfried replied absently, worried about his blood brother Gunther, who remained sunk in melancholy. Siegfried turned to Hagen. 'Is it Brünnhilde who troubles him?' he asked.

'If only,' said Hagen, 'he could understand her, as you understand birdsong.'

'Ah,' said Siegfried, 'I have heard women singing. I have forgotten the song of birds.'

'But you knew it once,' persisted Hagen. Siegfried was once again at Gunther's side. 'What can I do to pull you out of your gloom? Shall I tell you the stories of my youth?'

'Gladly,' said Gunther.

'Tell us,' said Hagen.

So Siegfried sat down on a rock and everyone crowded round to listen. Siegfried told them of his childhood with the evil Mime, of the smithy in the forest and of how the dwarf brought him up to be strong enough to slay a dragon who guarded an immense, age-old treasure. He told them of the fragments of his father's sword and the forging of Nothung. He told them of Neidhöle and the great fight when he had slain the dragon. He told them how the dragon's blood had burned his fingers and how, when he sucked them, he had suddenly understood the songs of the birds. He told them of the wood bird, who sang of the Tarnhelm which would lead him on to amazing adventures, and of the Ring which would make him master of the world.

'And did you take the Tarnhelm and the Ring?' prompted Hagen.

'I took them,' said Siegfried. And then he told them of the treachery of Mime and the poisoned drink and of how he slew Mime. Then Hagen offered him a drink from his horn, saying, 'I have mixed a herb in it which will awake your memories of these far-off deeds even more clearly.'

Siegfried's Funeral March

Siegfried gazed into the drinking horn, all unaware that it was as fatal as the draught which had enslaved him to Gutrune. Then he drank deeply from it and plunged deeply into the story of the fire-guarded rock and how he strode through the fire to find the beautiful Brünnhilde and of their instant fiery passion.

Gunther was on his feet in a flash. 'What am I hearing?' he cried.

Two black ravens rose from the bushes around, circled over Siegfried and flew steadily towards the Gibichung castle. Hagen calmly asked Siegfried if he could understand the speech of ravens too. Siegfried stood to watch the flight of the ravens, and as his back was turned Hagen shouted, 'To me they cried vengeance,' and plunged his spear deep into Siegfried's back.

Gunther and the vassals were horrified. 'Hagen, what have you done?'

But Hagen merely said, 'I have avenged treachery and a broken oath.' And he strode away. Siegfried lay dying but his only whispered words were to Brünnhilde. As if in a fever, he wished that she be re-awoken by his own kisses, her eyes sparking with love. Even in death, so dreaded and yet suddenly so welcome, he felt the greatest happiness of all – Brünnhilde's blessing.

Gunther and his vassals lifted the dead Siegfried onto his shield and carried him in solemn procession down to the Gibichung hall.

Back in the hall it was already night. Gutrune paced back and forth, desperately listening for sound of Siegfried's horn. She had had bad dreams, Grane neighing wildly and the sound of Brünnhilde's laughter. Who was it, she wondered, whom she saw go down to the river bank. Was it Brünnhilde? 'Brünnhilde frightens me,' she whispered to herself. She crept to Brünnhilde's chamber and looked in, calling softly, 'Are you awake?' The room was empty. And still no sound of Siegfried's horn. Only silence.

And then came the sound of Hagen's voice, growing nearer. 'Lights! Lights! Light up the torches! The hunters are home! Up Gutrune! Siegfried is home!'

As Hagen strode in, Gutrune rushed to him crying, 'What has happened? I never heard his horn.'

'Your pale hero will blow it no more,' said Hagen brutally. 'Not to the fair women, not to the hunt, not to battle.'

The vassals, in the torchlight, brought the corpse of Siegfried into the hall. 'What are they bringing here?' asked Gutrune.

'Prey', replied Hagen, 'the prey of a wild boar. Siegfried, your dead husband.'

Gutrune screamed and threw herself across the body. Gunther was at her side. 'Look up dear sister,' he begged, 'look at me, speak to me.' But Gutrune was inconsolable.

'Siegfried slain,' she howled. 'Faithless brother, murderer! O woe, they have slain Siegfried.'

'Do not rail at me,' cried Gunther. 'Hagen there, he is the boar that slew the hero.'

'Are you angry at that?' asked Hagen calmly.

Gunther raged at him, 'May you be hounded by evil and terror for ever!'

'Very well then, it was I, Hagen, who slew him. My spear was his destiny, the spear on which he swore the oath that he betrayed. And by the sacred laws of booty, here before you all, I now claim the Ring.'

Brünnhilde and Grane leap into the pyre

Gunther sprang out before him. 'Get back! What falls to me by right, that you shall never take from me!'

Hagen appealed to the vassals, 'Judge you then my right.' Gunther was beside himself. 'Do you dare to claim Gutrune's inheritance, you shameless son of Alberich?'

Hagen drew his sword. 'See how the son of Alberich demands his right!' And he launched himself upon Gunther. Gunther struggled to defend himself but was swiftly slain.

'Mine is the Ring!' cried Hagen and he strode towards the Ring that still rested on Siegfried's finger. As he approached, the hand of the dead Siegfried rose menacingly toward him. Hagen, terrified, staggered back, and everyone in the hall gasped in horror.

Suddenly the commanding figure of Brünnhilde was in their midst. 'Enough of your wailing,' she called out. 'All I have heard is the sound of children crying to their mother, never a lament worthy of the loss of the noblest of all heroes.'

Gutrune turned on her. 'Brünnhilde, consumed as you are with jealousy, it was you who roused these men against him. Woe that you ever came to this hall.'

But Brünnhilde turned on her with fury. 'Silence, wretched woman! You were never his wife, merely his mistress. I am his true consort. Siegfried and I swore our eternal vows before he ever set eyes on you.'

Gutrune, aware of her own guilt, cursed Hagen for giving her the drink that had stolen Siegfried from his true love, from Brünnhilde. She turned away in misery. 'Siegfried was never mine,' she whispered.

Brünnhilde commanded the Gibichung vassals to pile all the fire logs of the castle into a mighty funeral pyre for the greatest of all heroes. 'And bring his horse here, for he and I long to share Siegfried's highest and final honour.'

The vassals obeyed without a murmur. As the great pyre began to rise, Brünnhilde sank deep into reflection, and her thoughts were half for herself and half for her father, the wisest and mightiest of the gods. 'Like the clearest sunshine,' she mused, 'his light shone upon me. He was the purest of all beings, he who betrayed me. False to his wife, but true to his friends, he thwarted himself of his only love with his sword. No man ever swore more loyally, no man was ever more faithful to his vows, no man was ever purer in his love. Yet no man has ever betrayed his loyalty, his vows and his love, like him.'

Then she turned towards Valhalla and spoke directly to the gods. 'How came these things to be?' she demanded. 'Siegfried performed the greatest of all deeds, as you wished, and then you doomed him with the very curse which had doomed you. He, the truest of all heroes, was doomed to betray me that I might learn wisdom. Well, your wisdom I have learnt. I see it all clearly now. I hear the rustling of your raven's wings, Wotan. Your ravens I send back to you, with the tidings you have desired and yet feared for so long.'

Then she signed to the vassals to lift the body of Siegfried onto the pyre. From his finger she drew the fatal Ring, saying 'My accursed heritage I now take for my own. And thus I give it away. Dear and wise sisters of the river, you Rhinemaidens, I thank you for your counsel, and I give you out of my ashes the Ring you have missed for so long. Let the fire that will burn me, burn away its curse. Dissolve the curse in the waters of your river, and guard

Hagen is drowned and the Ring is restored

eternally the Gold whose theft wrought such evil.'

She took a flaming fire brand from the vassals. 'Fly home, you ravens,' she cried, 'fly over Brünnhilde's rock where Loge's fire still flames. Bid Loge fly to Valhalla, for now comes on the end of the gods. For look, the brand I throw is the brand that will consume Valhalla's proud battlements.'

The two great ravens rose majestically in the dusk and took wing towards the heights above.

Brünnhilde hurled the flaming torch onto the pyre, which burst into a blaze. Then she turned to her horse, Grane. 'Come my friend and companion, there lies your master, let us join him in the laughter of those flames. Already I burn with desire to greet him, to clasp him in my arms. We are all in the power of love.'

For the last time the great Valkyrie war cry rang out. 'Hei-a-ja-ho' called Brünnhilde, as she leapt onto the horse's back. With one gigantic leap Grane and Brünnhilde soared into the flames and were consumed in an instant.

As the Ring, still glittering, spiralled down towards the river from the ashes of Siegfried and Brünnhilde, the Rhine rose in a mighty surge, overflowing its banks, and on the crest of the wave were the three Rhinemaidens. Out of the fire and smoke dashed Hagen, crying, 'keep away from the Ring,' and plunged headlong after it into the flood. But Woglinde and Wellgunde just twined their arms around him and drew him inexorably down to his death in the depths of the river, leaving their sister Flosshilde to seize the Ring and hold it up triumphantly to the rays of the emerging sun. The fire of the huge funeral pyre seemed now to have engulfed the earth. The Gibichung hall disappeared in the conflagration and, far above, the vast towers of Valhalla exploded into flames. The two ravens circled and circled as the gods and their citadel melted into a furnace of destruction beneath them.

The sun came up and cast its golden blessing on the earth. The river subsided and the haunts of men and gods stood as blackened skeletons of their former power and pride. It seemed as if a great redemption had been granted to the earth. The gods, and their helpless mortal creations, together with hate, and spite, and jealousy and vengeance, had been purged away. Except for Alberich.

So the story ends as the Rhine flows majestically along, the Rhinemaidens afloat in it, singing ecstatically of the beauty and the magic of the Rhinegold. And somewhere, far below, in Nibelheim, the deepest pit of the earth, lurks Alberich, the embodiment of all evil.

Do you remember the beginning of this story…?

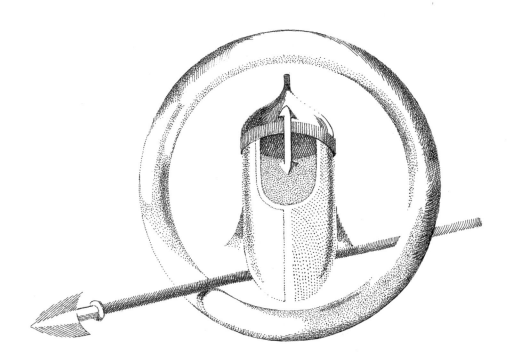